Change Management Leadership - Biblical Perspective

Author: Dr. Michael Teng

Published in 2011 by

Corporate Turnaround Centre Pte Ltd.

Printed in Singapore

By JCS Digital Solutions Pte Ltd

TABLE OF CONTENTS

Table of Contents

About the Author.. 8
Chapter 1 – LOOKING FOR LEADERSHIP 10
   Introduction... 10
     Leadership.. 10
     Where are Leaders Found? 11
   Leaders or Followers?... 11
   How Effective are Today's Leaders? 12
   What is a Social Entrepreneur?... 12
   The Financial Crisis and Global Recession 13
   An International Response to a Changing World... 14
   Who is Responsible for Checking the Patient's Pulse? 15
Chapter 2 – AN OVERVIEW OF GLOBAL LEADERSHIP..................................... 17
   Introduction... 17
   Great Historical Leaders 18
   Leadership in the West.. 18
   Leadership around the Globe 19
   Social Entrepreneurship on the Rise 20
   Leadership and Religion 20
Turbulent Times Need Inspired Leaders 22
Chapter 3 – MODELS OF LEADERSHIP 24
   Academic Leadership Models.. 24
     House's Path-Goal Theory.. 24
     Trait Theories 25
     Behavioural Theories 25
     Contingency Theories 25
     Power and Influence Theories, including Transactional Leadership 26
   More Recent Leadership Studies 27
     Shared Vision 28

Valuing Human Resources 28

Transformational Leadership 28

Characteristics of Leaders of Change 29

Communicators and Listeners 29

Leaders of Change are Proactive 30

Leaders of Change are Risk Takers 30

Summary: the Characteristics of Effective Leaders 30

Chapter 4 – A REVIEW OF MANAGEMENT THEORIES 32

Frederick Taylor against the Captains of Industry 33

Max Weber and Henri Fayol – Bureaucratic Management 33

Elton Mayo and the Human Relations Movement 34

Modern Theories 34

From Management to Leadership 34

Leadership in a Changing World 35

Chapter 5 – MANAGEMENT AND CRISIS MANAGEMENT 37

Overview 37

Crisis Leadership and Crisis Management 37

WICH Management Structure 37

How Conflict can Reshape Companies 38

Crisis and the Leader 38

The 80/20 Principle 39

Psychology of Business 39

Maximum Exertion of Powers 40

Chapter 6 – LEADERSHIP AND CRISIS 41

Abraham and Moses 41

Non-Biblical leaders 42

Defining great leadership 43

Change Management Leadership – A Biblical Perspective 46

Chapter 7 – LEARNING LEADERSHIP THROUGH FAITH 48

David: Surviving Adversity and Success with Humility 48

Elisha's Self-Sacrificing Spirit 49

Gideon and the 300 49

Moses and Crisis Management 50

Noah, a Man of Action 51

Nebuchadnezzar's Pride and Failure 51
Joab: the Right Place for Glory.. 51
Jeremiah Does the Right Thing for the Business.. 52
Samuel: from Humble Beginnings to Success.. 52
Paul's Quest for the Truth 52
Chapter 8 – The "Corporate Turnaround" Model for Change 54
Where is Your Company Heading?... 54
Corporate Turnaround: The Map for the Journey.. 54
Introduction to the "Corporate Turnaround" Model for Change 54
Surgery Phase: To Cut is to Cure 55
Resuscitation Phase.. 55
Nursing Phase 56
Chapter 9 – Phase One: SURGERY: The Autocratic Leader........................... 57
A Company in Need of Surgery... 57
Change Management Leadership for the Surgery Phase 57
Internal and External Causes of Corporate Disease... 57
The Steps of Surgery... 57
Communicate 58
Concentrate 58
Control Costs 58
Control Cash Flow 58
Joshua, an Autocratic Leader 59
Chapter 10 – Phase Two: RESUSCITATION: The Democratic Leader............ 61
Resuscitating Your Company through Short-Term Projects................................ 61
Change Management Leadership for the Resuscitation Phase 61
Primary Steps in the Resuscitation Phase 61
Determine Corporate Objectives... 61
Keep it Real.. 62
Develop the Right Product at the Right Price 62
Implement an Aggressive Marketing Strategy... 62
Differentiate using Service Quality 63
Strengthen the Brand Name 63
Invest in Future Expansion 64
King David, the Democratic Leader 64

Chapter 11 – Phase Three: NURSING: The Corporate Man 67

Phase Three: The Nursing Stage: The Corporate Man 67

Change Management Leadership for the Nursing Phase 67

Twin Approaches During the Resuscitation Phase 67

Nursing a Corporation through Philosophy 67

Seek New Concepts and Methods.. 68

Appreciate On-going Change 68

Accept Some Failure.. 68

Nursing a Corporation through Action 69

Changing a Corporate Culture 69

The Apostle Paul as the Corporate Man 70

Paul's Resume.. 70

Paul as a Corporate Role Model 71

Chapter 12 – The Dimensional Shift: The Greatest Leader.. 73

Dimensional Shift: Jesus, the Greatest Leader 73

How Jesus Met Various Needs.. 73

Jesus Worked with a Variety of People 73

How Jesus Worked with Small Teams and Large Crowds.. 74

Jesus and the Corporate Turnaround Process.. 74

Jesus in the Surgery Phase: Decisive Leadership 74

Jesus in the Resuscitation Phase: Compassionate but Fair 75

Jesus in the Nursing Phase: Building a Better Future.. 75

Cultural Change 75

Jesus Spoke for Cultural Change 75

Jesus Acted for Cultural Change.. 76

Jesus Provided Leadership to Meet the Need 76

Chapter 13 – Conclusion: Managing Change: Tested and True.. 77

Change Management Leadership and Biblical Examples 77

Leaders, Managers and Leadership.. 77

Corporate Turnaround Requires Change Management.. 77

Leadership is about Character as well as Skill.. 77

Tested and True Business Management and Biblical Management.. 78

About the Author

Dr. Teng is widely recognized as a turnaround CEO in Asia by the news media. He has been interviewed on the international media on many occasions on the subject of corporate turnaround and transformation as well as Internet marketing such as the Malaysian Business Radio, BFM 89-9, News Radio FM 93.8, Malaysian Business Radio, Edge Radio (USA), the Channel News Asia, the Boss Magazine, Economic Bulletin, the Today, World Executive Digest, Lianhe ZaoPao, StarBiz and the Straits Times. Success University and SkyquestCom broadcast his online seminars globally to 120 countries.

Dr. Mike Teng is the author of a best-selling book *"Corporate Turnaround: Nursing a Sick Company Back to Health"*, in 2002 which is also translated into the Bahasa, Indonesia and Mandarin. Management guru Professor Philip Kotler and business tycoons Mr. Oei Hong Leong and Dr. YY Wong endorse his book. He has subsequently authored more than nineteen management books. Three of the books are on Internet marketing.

Dr. Teng is currently the Managing Director of Corporate Turnaround Centre Pte Ltd (www.corporateturnaroundcentre.com), which provides corporate training and management advisory services in Singapore, Malaysia, Vietnam, Ghana, etc. He is the national trainer appointed by the Singapore government to train displaced senior managers and deploy them to run SMEs.

He has more than 29 years of experience in starting new plants, strategic planning, and operational management responsibilities in the Asia Pacific region. Of these, he held Chief Executive Officer positions for 19 years in multi-national and publicly listed companies. He was the CEO of a U.S. MNC based in Singapore for ten years. He spearheaded the turnaround of several troubled companies. He also advised several boards of directors of publicly listed companies.

Dr. Teng served as an Executive Council member for fourteen years and the last four years as the President of the Marketing Institute of Singapore (2000 – 2004), the national marketing association. He is the President of the National University Singapore MBA Alumni and University of South Australia Alumni.

Dr. Teng holds a Doctorate in Business Administration (DBA) from the University of South Australia, a Master of Business Administration (MBA) and Bachelor of Mechanical Engineering (BEng) from the National University of Singapore. He is also a Professional Engineer (P Eng, Singapore), Chartered Engineer (C Eng, UK) and Fellow Member of several prestigious professional institutes, namely Chartered Institute of Marketing (FCIM), Chartered Management Institute (FCMI), Institute of Mechanical Engineers (FIMechE), Marketing Institute of Singapore (FMIS), Institute of Electrical Engineers (FIEE) and Senior Member of Singapore Computer Society (SMSCS). He is also a Practising Management Consultant (PMC) certified by the Singapore government.

Chapter 1 – LOOKING FOR LEADERSHIP

Introduction

This book describes the leadership necessary to manage organizational change successfully. We begin with an overview of leadership styles. We also look briefly at challenges currently faced by different organizations, both in business and in politics. These challenges clearly show that organizations need radical change to survive in these turbulent times. To do so will require great leadership.

The primary focus of this book is the leadership required for change management. This involves knowing what changes to make, and in what sequence. It also requires specific leadership skills and qualities, beyond general skills in "business management". We take inspiration from several leaders found in the Bible, because they overcame a variety of severe challenges during different historic epochs and because of the enormous impact they made. Some leaders from other cultures and situations are also noted.

If the going is easy, a business can survive with a caretaker CEO: a person who simply manages the company. During our turbulent times, an enterprise needs a leader with a vision of what the future should be, as well as the skills to make that future a reality.

An organization in trouble needs radical change, much as a dying patient might need medical treatment. Are corporations in such ill health that radical surgery is required? This book will explore what change management leadership can do for your organization.

Leadership

Leaders and leadership skills attract an unending stream of criticism and speculation. Different strategies are required to cope with the changes that this social climate requires. There is constant hope that new leaders will emerge, who recognize these social changes and have the ability to do something about them. The financial crisis affecting the world needs forward thinkers to recognize the effect these financial problems are likely to have on social responsibility. Despite the crisis that has arisen within the financial world, there still seems to be the idea that leaders are going to rise up to meet the challenges waiting to be thrust upon them and have the ability to guide the world out of the recession it has found itself in.

Leadership skills of those accountable for conducting those changes have regularly come under intense and persistent examination from the media. The academic world has also been probing "management and "leadership" for at least a century. Both are interested in establishing what it is that makes a superior leader. The popular press focuses their attention on the critical roles that leaders play. They attempt to establish the characteristics that enable these leaders to introduce and maintain successful changes. This chapter focuses on the characteristics of these leaders. It also looks at those drivers of change and tries to find out whether these leaders share similar characteristics. This chapter also aims to establish which characteristics, if any, are unique to specific roles.

Where are Leaders Found?

Many effective leaders are found in the Bible. This chapter attempts to determine the characteristics that may help or hinder corporate leaders who appear to be shaping events on the world stage. Globalization, information and communication technology and climatic change will also be investigated. Can effective leadership skills be attributed to personal leadership practices? In this chapter the study of leadership skills seeks to identify what personal attributes are exhibited from the context of the Bible.

This chapter provides a brief review of some of the key leadership concepts, taken within the context of the corporate world of today. It seeks to establish who we are in the present scheme of things and where events currently stand on the world stage. In this chapter we focus on our leaders' need for change, taken within the current leadership situation. Today's financial crisis is discussed as well as the way our leaders of today have handled this critical issue, taking into account individual players on the World stage: the EU, US, UK, China, India and South Africa.

This chapter provides a discussion about those countries' response to a changing world. Also investigated is change that has been forced through, as opposed to planned change. This chapter introduces the concept of whether there is a link between today's drivers for change, together with leadership challenge and a divine purpose to events that are shaping our world today. During this chapter there will be a discussion on the Bible as being the most appropriate leadership manual. The discussion will also show how the Bible can be used to shape our future leaders into making more appropriate change policies that could result in more beneficial events.

The information contained within this chapter is intended for leaders involved with influencing system-wide changes at the corporate level. Information within this chapter is intended to be of value to those training potential leaders. It is intended for those arranging and carrying out training programs that are going to influence the leaders of change. The information in this chapter is also intended to shape the events that will change our futures. Finally, this chapter attempts to raise the awareness amongst individuals who promote corporate change in accordance with biblical principles.

Leaders or Followers?

There appear to be distinct personality differences between leaders and followers, a fact recognized by various studies that have been carried out since the 1900s. However, despite no end of research, it still has not been possible to establish exactly what that elusive 'something' is that makes an effective leader.

Various academic theories have been proposed, tested and, to some degree, found wanting. Stogdill claims that it takes more than just a combination of character traits. Hencley and others found that the social situation, including an organization's structure and the current necessity, helps to create leaders. By the middle 1960s, the studies were coming to some consensus that some combination of personal characteristics and the environment was required to create leadership behaviours.

So far, the result of all this thinking about what produces the best kinds of leaders seemed to lead researchers towards the conclusion that the best kinds of leaders can balance the requirements of both the tasks needed within the organization with the human needs and requirements to achieve a fulfilled workforce and get all the tasks done adequately and within an appropriate time-frame.

How Effective are Today's Leaders?

Are our leaders particularly effective in today's world? Have our leaders, by their own actions, contributed towards the financial recession from which our world is slowly emerging? Are there any leaders today who are strong enough to lead the world forward into a new age? On the other hand, are any leaders emerging with a completely different attitude and approach?

One of today's most eminent leaders, according to the US News and World Report in 2005, is Bill Drayton. He is the founder of Ashoka, a company that provides entrepreneurial solutions around the globe. Bill Drayton's vision of social responsibility led to his ideas being introduced in over 60 countries through his network of Ashoka Fellows, all social entrepreneurs who each have a profound effect within their local areas. They may not be building multinational corporations, but perhaps CEOs can learn valuable lessons from the priorities and methods used by these social entrepreneurs.

By 2011, traditional politics has become ineffective or unrecognizable in a number of countries and situations. A minor example may be the serious loss of seats by the federal Liberal party of Canada in the 2011 election; will that party re-invent itself and return to power? That election broke a logjam of minority governments in Canada; Australia currently is ruled by a coalition government.

An amazing and radical shift is playing out in the "Arab Awakening" in the spring of 2011. Several countries in the Middle East have seen regimes "under attack" by socially-networked young adults. Their traditional leaders are carefully stepping away from entrenched positions of privilege and authority so as to accommodate change with minimal disruption. Libya provides a counter-example, where the leader clings to power by force in the face of international military intervention.

The United States made a radical change in president, but Obama has continued or fulfilled missions undertaken by his ideologically-opposed predecessors. The recent killing of Osama bin-Laden, as well as the USA's military participation with NATO in Libya, do not seem radically different from what Presidents Bush (Senior and Junior) would have chosen to do.

Japan, Thailand, Malaysia and Singapore have either seen a change of leader or a loss of popular support for their ruling governments.

For all those situations, the questions of change management leadership are: Is that country in the midst of change? Are the political leaders managing those changes, or are they being driven by forces they neither understand nor control?

What is a Social Entrepreneur?

There is certainly no shortage of social problems around the world that need good leaders, dedicated to relieving some of the burdens placed on societies everywhere. No country is without its social problems, whether that country is struggling to find their place within the global economy or whether the country is an established Western power with more local threats to stability.

Social entrepreneurs recognize and act to alleviate some of the burdens, recognizing that many of these problems cannot be surmounted in ways that have been tried in the past. New ways are needed for a new society, especially as some of these problems are occurring as the result of the new society that is emerging. This calls for new leaders who are dedicated and far-sighted enough to focus on what actually needs to be done and then finding new ways in which they can help. They do not necessarily build economic empires for their own profit; but they do not expect to fund unprofitable projects through an unending stream of donations, either.

Social entrepreneurs think up new ways to actually change the system from within, finding answers from amongst the communities involved, then leading these communities towards a solution. For this, these leaders need to be dedicated, be supportive and have adequate support themselves. Ashoka provides that support, so that Ashoka Fellows can dedicate their lives to changing directions and empowering communities to help themselves. Social entrepreneurs are role models and facilitators. These are the leaders of change for the masses: leaders with a social conscience who provide ethical support to as many people in a community who will then be empowered to make changes and continue with the work that was started with Ashoka's help.

It would have been quite easy to introduce various political leaders, presidents and sovereigns, but invariably many of these are far too far removed from the people at ground level to make much of an impression to individual people and communities. Politicians, presidents and sovereigns lead from the top, but in today's world, to make a real difference, change needs to happen from within – from the communities themselves who are actually experiencing the problems first-hand.

Even a CEO of a for-profit corporation might do well to consider the aims and means of social entrepreneurs. One example is Jack Welch, who decentralized decision-making at General Electric in the 1960s. By removing many layers of bureaucracy, Welch released the creativity of GE's design engineers. This led to an explosion of new inventions and new products.

"Internal Entrepreneurship" is a concept that periodically comes into favour in management circles and then fades; but it was demonstrated at GE under Welch.

Another view of "social entrepreneurship" sees the opportunity to partner with trade unions. One might seek cooperation from the unions to keep onshore factories open, rather than sending the work off-shore. This approach seeks a win-win solution for existing employees, as well as competitive improvements for the company through greater flexibility in contracts.

The Financial Crisis and Global Recession

The economy in the USA represents perhaps 20% of the global economy. As a result, when the economy looks bad in the US, soon the rest of the world begins to feel the effects. According to the definition provided by the United States, a recession occurs when economic activity is significantly reduced for more than just six months. This depressed economy is usually represented in real terms when it has an effect on people's income, employment, retail sales and industrial activity. The recession has been attributed to a credit crisis, but that is rather a simplistic explanation because nothing happens in isolation, not even a recession.

Some have attributed the overall cause of the recession to fraud. It was certainly the reason for the collapse of Washington Mutual according to the conclusions reached by an investigation into the reason the largest commercial bank collapsed. A report published on 13th April 2010 attributes Washington Mutual's pay structure to be the overall reason for the collapse of the bank. However, according to this report, their pay structure had the overall effect of toxic mortgages being dumped into the financial market. Lehman Brothers also contributed to the credit crisis according to another investigation whose report was also published on that same day in the *New York Times*.

The recession eventually rolled around the world, fuelled by innumerable other events that attributed towards the snowball effect of the recession. Iceland's banks also succumbed to pressures felt as the recession rolled past. An investigation that looked into irregular activities of some of Iceland's government leaders, reported they should be held accountable for 'gross negligence'. As a result the whole of Iceland's banking system failed, along with its government. Many other key figures were taken down alongside this downfall. It is not just the US and Iceland that were affected, but events occurring in both these countries had profound effects on banking systems around the world, with repercussions still reverberating today. Government leaders are attempting to make considerable sums of money available to help prop up failing industry in the hopes of getting unemployed back into work. This will not happen overnight and recovery is going to take some time.

An International Response to a Changing World

Since the formation of new countries and the emergence of new nations in the late 1940s and the opening up of the Western Bloc during the late 1980s and 1990s the world has been in a constant state of flux. The world is changing, with the shift from individual trading borders to truly liberated global industrialization. This has coincided, to a certain extent, with the development of the World Wide Web. When it comes to the financial sector and the movement of goods around the world, it is truly becoming a market without boundaries. Much as this is a good thing, it is causing international re-alignments, with nations such as China and India emerging as countries that, economically, are becoming true powers in their own right.

Alongside this changing world is the emergence of global terrorism that appears to be uniting nations rather than severing alliances. The role of the United States is altering on the world stage, becoming more dependent on establishing and maintaining good relationships with other countries. No longer can the USA rely on her size to intimidate other powers as India and China are both waiting in the wings to mount a rear-guard action. There has been sustained economic growth in both India and China, with both countries remaining buoyant during the economic downturn experienced in the West during 2009. Both countries have a young population, which translates into an eager and able workforce.

The economy in Brazil is also shaping up nicely, ready to take a slice of the global economy. Indonesia's economy is growing steadily, as well. At the moment the Euro is causing concern in the EEC countries, with Greece certainly still struggling financially. Turkey is waiting to see what happens with the single currency economy before making a final decision whether or not to scrap the Turkish Lira. An ageing population is one of the major drawbacks many of the European countries face. Another problem is the issue of immigration. Both the education and the tax systems need to make the European countries more appealing to attract a willing workforce. A younger population is something that is desperately needed if the EU countries are to maintain their position amidst the global economy.

Of all the Asian countries, Japan faces an ageing workforce itself and coping with the aftermath of the major earthquake in 2011. The only way Japan's economic recovery can continue is to ally itself to one of its neighbours. Despite the upswing in Asia's economy and their chance to become a major player on the global economic stage, North Korea's simmering problems could, at any time, explode and hamper the healthy economy of its neighbouring countries. Meanwhile, Russia holds a strategic position as a giant oil and gas exporter, yet it has yet to respond to the shifting alliances of the 21st century. Russia's medical care is poor. As a country its infrastructure, over the expanse of the vast continent, needs to be fully restructured. It has social problems and a low birth rate. This is not a recipe for economic growth although some of its satellite countries are eager to take over and contribute economically to the demographic shift of allegiances and alliances.

Who is Responsible for Checking the Patient's Pulse?

There is no doubt about it: the economic climate at present certainly needs a period of convalescence. To recover, the economy needs to function as a globalised unit. The days of individual wrangles between countries are as obsolete as the minor kingdoms and princedoms of Europe in the Middle Ages. It is time for the leading economies to function as a unit. Each individual country has their own independent function and social responsibility related to the local communities within each country. However, just as the Body of Christ was designed by God to work as a single unit, these individual countries need to contribute towards the economic benefit on a global scale. For these countries to achieve this unity they need to acknowledge that they are accountable.

Accountability is all about liability and being answerable for any activities undertaken. Once accountability has been established it provides much greater protection and ensures any leader is answerable for their actions. Consider what has been said about power and accountability by some leading thinkers from the past.

The nineteenth century historian, John Emerich Edward Dalberg Acton, was attributed in 1887 with quoting to Bishop Mandell Creighton: "*Power tends to corrupt, and absolute power corrupts absolutely. Great men are almost always bad men*".

Something similar was said by British Prime Minister, William Pitt the Elder in 1770, in a speech he made to the House of Lords: "*Unlimited power is apt to corrupt the minds of those who possess it*".

There is no room in today's global society for powerful leaders not to be accountable for their actions. God expects accountability, as stated in Romans 14: 12: "*So then each of us shall give account of himself to God*".

The world is full of sin and temptation, which makes accountability all the more important. In Ephesians 6:12, Paul is writing a letter to the Church in Ephesus. In his letter to them he reinforces the need for accountability to ensure that you win the battle against sin: "*For our struggle is not against flesh and blood, but against the rulers, against the authorities, against the powers of this dark world and against the spiritual forces of evil in the heavenly realms*".

Accountability is a safety net to prevent us from slipping from the path of truth and honesty. To continue the doctor/patient analogy: how do we ensure that an ambulance attendant does not steal the wallet from an unconscious patient? How do we make a doctor accountable for providing the proper care?

This chapter's main focus was on individual leadership, and how effective one leader can be in a larger context. The context for that leadership was economics and business. The next chapter will examine other large organizations: how effective have political, business or religious leaders been on the global stage?

Chapter 2 – AN OVERVIEW OF GLOBAL LEADERSHIP

Introduction

Even if some corporations experience difficulties, surely there are politicians or religious leaders on the global stage who could serve as examples of the leadership required to revive organizations in distress. How effective are some of the leaders found on the world stage, either currently or in the past?

Many of these opinions are quoted from well-regarded sources. It is important to realize that so many people have recognized the problems with current global leadership.

Less than three years ago, in 2008, the financial world was in shambles. Would the global financial system collapse? Would it turn into a global trade crisis? What are the appropriate responses by governments and financial institutions? How should individual businesses redefine their strategies?

One thing was sure, even then: the situation would affect nearly every business in the world. And it did. Much more in certain sectors and countries than others, but it was felt in every corner of the globe. The greatest threat seemed to be increased protectionism. The atmosphere was eased a bit in 2008, when the G20 declared they would refrain from any measures to hinder the export of goods or services.[1]

But it did not do much to support countless enterprises whose order books turned empty almost overnight, particularly in developing markets. Expansion investments were halted or cancelled, workers were set on half time workloads, and panic was all around. A few months later, even more draconian measures needed to be taken: foreclosures abounded, as many businesses could not repay their bank loans, and many employees lost their jobs. Cost cutting was often the only way to keep the company alive for the short term.

But management was often very insecure about the long term. This was a deep crisis, and a rebound of the global economy was not going to come soon. So, what actions must be taken, and in what direction? Some sources still indicated a positive outlook, expressing faith in globalization.[2] Others saw a leadership crisis, calling for political and business leaders to be responsible for getting positive results in the right way: sustainably and with transparency.

I am not convinced that indeed the global financial crisis can be reduced to a leadership problem, but have to agree it is a major contributing part. And it is definitely in the right direction: the 'economy', however substantive, is nothing more than the framework and the product of what has been produced by 'people'. Without people there is no economy. And the 'leaders' are the

---

[1]**G20 2008** - Declaration Summit on Financial Markets and the World Economy.
http://www.g20.org/Documents/g20_summit_declaration.pdf
[2]**McKinsey 2010** - McKinsey Quarterly, 'Five forces reshaping the global economy: McKinsey Global Survey results', May 2010.
https://www.mckinseyquarterly.com/Five_forces_reshaping_the_global_economy_McKinsey_Global_Survey_results_2581

ones who drive the economy, whether they are at the steering wheel of countries, organizations or enterprises. And so their current leadership will shape the economy of tomorrow.

Great Historical Leaders

Looking back in history, some names keep popping up: Augustus Caesar, Charlemagne, Genghis Khan, Napoleon Bonaparte, Franklin Roosevelt, Abraham Lincoln, Winston Churchill, Adolf Hitler, Mohandas Gandhi, Mao Tse Tung, Nelson Mandela, Jesus. You may well not all agree about such a list, or over the outcome, but even if some of them failed miserably at some time in their life, the fact remains that they were great leaders. They had tremendous impact on the people around them, and that is exactly what makes a great leader. All of them have built an 'empire' – not necessarily always in geographical terms – and had uncountable followers – sometimes, as is the case of Jesus, only generations later.

Leadership in the West

The USA is probably the country where most has been written about leadership and management styles. It has not only produced an impressive list of professors and gurus on the subject – who has not heard of Peter Drucker, Warren Bennis and John Kotter – but its political system has also led to a continuous scrutiny of its national leaders. With each new president, the expectations on supreme leadership are very high, perhaps too high.

With the election of Barack Obama as the new president, the focus on leadership again was high in the news. The presidential campaign, which lasted almost two years, was executed with near-perfection, a *'flawless model of consistency and discipline'* one could read in the Boston Globe[3]. But unlike the campaign, which is a well-orchestrated machine, being in charge can be lonely, as one faces public opinion on one side, and a vested bureaucracy on the other. And that has clearly shown. After one year of presidency, Internet blogs as well as newspapers produced headings such as *'Obama fails the test of leadership'* (Politico, June 3, 2010), *'Obama's Leadership Vacuum'* (The Heritage Foundation blog, June 23, 2010), *'Obama's Leadership Crisis'* (The Daily Caller, June 7, 2010). (One may argue that many of these attacks are made by partisans, rather than by disinterested observers. Regardless, these attacks may well shape public opinion).
In business likewise, a series of 'management gurus' has emerged. Who can forget GE's legend Jack Welch, or in more recent times, Bill Gates? Back in 2003, Fortune Magazine published an interesting The 10 Greatest CEOs of All Time[4], which listed a few unexpected figures. In the first place we find Charles Coffin – a name many of you may never have heard of. He was GE's first president, and his greatness was exactly his humility. He knew very well he would not be the next Thomas Edison, and after him came a series of giants (Swope, Cordiner, Jones and Welch) that make it easy to overlook Coffin altogether. But it was Coffin who set the stage and built a system and a climate that ensured bringing out the greatness of the people he worked with, as well as of the generations of employees to come. On place 4 we have George Merck, *'the boss who didn't worry about Wall Street – and grew profits 50-fold'*. What marked him particularly was his attitude of 'medicine is for people, not for profits'. Several times, his company has

---

[3] The Boston Globe of January 17, 2009.
[4] Fortune Magazine, July 21, 2003, as described on:
http://money.cnn.com/magazines/fortune/fortune_archive/2003/07/21/346095/index.htm

distributed medications for free or at a low cost, to serve a social cause. After 30 years, a product like Mectizan is still saving millions of people each year, largely free of charge.

Both these last examples bring out the very essence of great leadership: persistence, inspiration, humility and value of ethics. It is these measurements that overshadow those of the traditional business KPI's such as turnover and profits, making 'leadership' stand out above 'management'.

Leadership around the Globe

The same basic qualities are to be met around the world.

Nelson Mandela cited his top three lessons of leadership as: to take courage from an inspiration; to use flexible tactics within persistent principles; and to humbly guide from behind so others feel empowered.

In the last years of British control over India, Mahatma (Mohandas) Gandhi was undoubtedly the political and spiritual leader of India, without ever having held any official position. And his inspirational influence extended well beyond the borders of India. Few leaders have inspired so many other leaders. And it would be a gigantic task to find a leader who displays an equal degree of humility. But this little, almost shy man was gifted with an unprecedented will and persistence, and loyalty to the ethical foundations he was brought up with. One of the main reasons behind Gandhi's reputed leadership is that it came from the bottom, not the top. He was driven by and sympathized with the poor and powerless masses, perhaps exemplified in his almost obsessive promotion of homespun cloth. While a clear reaction to the behaviour of India's elite – who imported their textiles from England – his devotion to homespun cloth was much more than a means to revive or protect employment of the poor. Wearing the traditional homespun cloth was a symbol of his dedication to the poor, as much as it was emphasizing his humble nature.

Leadership further east, as exemplified in Japan, is much more difficult to identify, because it is less public, or at least less visible. Individual leadership is seldom displayed, as leadership in Japan is of the participative kind. Although the leader – often "seniority" means "highest in age" – will make the final decision, it is never a one-man process. It is the result of seemingly endless consultation with everyone involved. The decision taken – or perhaps "made official" – by the leader, reflects the consensus of all subordinates. The same approach is true for a majority of South Asian and Southeast Asian countries. The process of 'seeking support of' and 'consensus with' the base will be beneficial for the 'harmony' or unity within the country, organization or company: a highly-valued aspect. Listing one's personal accomplishments – which would be positively valued in the USA – would have a distinctive negative effect in Japan, where modesty, humility and respect for the group (the business entity) are values expected and respected.

But do not let this lead you to the wrong conclusion that individuality would be lost in the group. Relationships are much more personal in the east than in the west. A business relationship can take years to develop, as it is intensely and closely tied up with the individuals involved. With the much more frequent job changes in the west, this can be seriously counterproductive: sending an 'other' VP Marketing on a business trip to Japan the following year (because the previous VP had quit and was replaced by an outsider), could very well mean that most of the relationship building process has to be started anew. In the Japanese company, even if the previous manager had retired, you would have certainly met the new one already during last year's negotiations, even if he were on a lower echelon. And if not, the 'old' one would be present during this year's meetings, even if no longer in function, just for the continuation of the relationship.

Social Entrepreneurship on the Rise

A relatively new phenomenon that is distinctly pushing through is social entrepreneurship. All too often identified with an institution such as Grameen Bank, which is certainly one of the most talked about, with a Nobel Peace Prize in 2006, the scope goes much further. Described as a type of entrepreneurship that focuses on social change, where the emphasis is not profit or return, but the creation of social capital, it was for a long time seen as associated with voluntary or not-for-profit activities. In recent years however, it has risen far beyond this, and grown out in the direction of 'normal' business ventures. At the same time, many 'normal' businesses have allocated an increasing importance to 'social responsibility', and who knows, these two evolutions might very well meet in the future.

Although the first experiments in social entrepreneurship came about in the late 1950s, the efforts of Ashoka, founded by Bill Drayton, and particularly the start of its 'Change makers' initiative, made it shoot through the roof in the 1980s and 1990s, making it at the beginning of this century a well-established alternative form of doing business. Although still a majority of initiatives are in the not-for-profit sector, including many NGO operations, several for-profit initiatives such as SKS Microfinance – an initiative of McKinsey alumnus Vikram Akula – are growing. Social entrepreneurship has flourished particularly well in South Asia (India and Bangladesh), and is spreading fast over most of the developing world.

To identify and start solving a moderate-to-large scale social problem requires an enormous amount of determination, persistence and vision. The benefits go to a group of often marginalized or disadvantaged people, who are not engaged in an employer-employee relationship, but often in a vendor-client relationship. That is, they are clients of the bank lending them a microfinance credit, being stimulated to become an entrepreneur on their own, being financed and coached by the vendor. The whole process is fundamentally a '*don't give them a fish, but teach them how to fish*' approach.

While the process is too young to change the way of global business, the results have already changed the life of millions of people, and are in some cases changing the political stage, and, to a certain extent, society.

Leadership and Religion

Although religion is often seen as the opposite of business, leadership has many similarities in both religion and business. The main characteristics of leadership mentioned above – persistence, inspiration, humility and value of ethics – are found back in all major religions, and vividly presented in their founders and original religious leaders.

Nobody will challenge the high value of ethics and highly inspirational character of these religious leaders, whether Buddha, Mohamed or Jesus. And that they were persistent in their way of viewing the world is equally evident. This characteristic is even present in the Buddha's birth name, Siddhartha, meaning 'he who achieves his aim'. But to some it might come as a surprise that all of them had a high degree of humility. Although known for preaching to larger crowds, more often than not, they called for restraint in promoting their teachings or deeds. When Jesus had healed a lame person or leper, he always sent him to present himself to the authorities 'to show that he was healed', but never asked him to publicize who was behind it, or how it happened. And if any reference was to be made to the case, it had to be attributed to the higher Power. In John 2:1-12, when solving the wine shortage at the wedding in Cana, Jesus instructed only the servants. He never interacted with the hosts, but, typically, remained on the background during the whole event.

Lord Buddha, even if of royal blood, lived a very simple and ascetic life, travelling by foot, and avoiding all expressions of luxury. Much less is known about the details of the Buddha's life compared to that of Jesus – probably because it is much farther in the past, the content of the texts are much more mythical in character – but at various places in the story, and from his preaching, there is no doubt about his humble attitude.

Of the personal life of Mohamed, even fewer details are known. He was born in a middle class family of traders. While orphaned at a very young age, he grew up in his uncle's house, and later, entered into the service of a rich businesswoman, Khadijah, to whom he finally got married. Although she was more than ten years older than he, it was a faithful and happy marriage, and, although polygamy was the norm, he never took another wife as long as Khadijah lived. As a fairly wealthy man, he lived in comfortable conditions but led a simple life as father of eight children, and husband of Khadijah. The remainder of all known biographies focus entirely on Islam-related events, and conceal any facts of a more personal nature concerning the Prophet.

This chapter moved from global corporations, through politicians, to the founders of major religions. Both businesses and religions affect the world. In these turbulent times, can a business leader be a positive influence for good? The next chapter surveys a variety of leadership styles.

Turbulent Times Need Inspired Leaders

It is easy to rule and make important decisions
When the profits are good and do not need incisions
It is easy to rule when good times are rocking
And criticisms of your style are not knocking

The times though have turned they are no longer good
The times have got rough, and profits are not as they should
The time for change management has arrived
The time for change management is not contrived

Chorus
Turbulent times call for leaders and inspiring people
Turbulent times are being shouted from the steeples
The world has changed and we must all stand as one
And leaders become heroes, and do what must be done

Some people are born to lead others to follow
But we all have a role and all want to wallow
In good times and a good world of prosperity
Which is peaceful and for all to love and see

Leaders such as President Obama are having a hard time
Leaders such as Bernanke are having to relearn their lines
For they recognise the need for change management
They recognise the old ways are just entanglement

Chorus
Turbulent times call for leaders and inspiring people
Turbulent times are being shouted from the steeples
The world has changed and we must all stand as one
And leaders become heroes, and do what must be done

Thinking and planning is the only way to succeed
In addressing the problems, addressing world need
If we look at things differently then we have the idea
If we look at things studiously, then answers are clear

Leaders everywhere face an economic crisis
Leaders everywhere face much economic unrest
But the good ones know the answers are in demand
The clever ones have them now, and are saving the land

Chorus
Turbulent times call for leaders and inspiring people

Turbulent times are being shouted from the steeples
The world has changed and we must all stand as one
And leaders become heroes, and do what must be done

Chapter 3 – MODELS OF LEADERSHIP

It would be tempting to move directly from the challenges outlined in the previous chapters, and present a tidy solution. Simply outline what must be done, and the type of person to manage those tasks, and this book would be complete.

First, however, we should consider the evolution of "leader ship models" within the academic community. Understanding how modern concepts of leadership have developed will help us to appreciate the criteria for the "leader" needed to implement change management.

Academic Leadership Models

Meanwhile, the search continued for the variables that could possibly identify leadership potential. Business strategists have pursued in academic studies and this quest since at least the 1930s. This topic is immense, but can be condensed by touching on the highlights in a more academic manner. A brief summary of the most helpful concepts follows.

House's Path-Goal Theory

One may focus on the character traits of a single leader. House's Path-Goal theory isolated four leadership qualities:
- Directive
- Achievement-orientated
- Supportive
- Participative

A "directive" leader gives specific instructions to subordinates. The "achievement-orientated" leader sets the goals but allows subordinates some freedom in determining the methods. A "supportive" leader includes the welfare of subordinates in making decisions and setting tasks. A "participative" leader consults with subordinates, seeking input and advice before making a final decision.

Furthermore, House identified two situational variables:

- The personal characteristics of those who were in subordinate positions
- The working environment, especially the rules and regulations of the organization.

Later theorists such as Barnes and Kriger suggested that an organization often sees different members of the management team offer their leadership at varying times and in response to changing circumstances.

Over the years four main classifications of leadership theories have emerged. These include:

- Trait Theories

- Behavioural Theories
- Contingency Theories
- Power and Influence Theories (sometimes seen as subordinate to Contingency)

The first of these groups refers to the best kind of person has the makings of a good leader. The second relates to the kinds of things a good leader does to establish that hierarchy. The third group refers to how circumstance may affect the quality of leadership. The final group explains the relationship between the accepted leader and the source of that actual recognition of leadership qualities.

Trait Theories

Probably the simplest way to describe the idea behind trait theories is the concept of "either you've got it or you haven't". That description is simplistic but helpful. According to Trait Theories, leaders have instinctive abilities to lead, thanks to their personalities or innate skills. The theories do not explain why followers instinctively recognize those qualities in that leader.

Trait theories are now obsolete, since people can be trained to take on leadership roles, or can emerge as leaders when circumstances change.

Behavioural Theories

Kurt Lewin was one of the better-known supporters of the Behavioural Theories during the 1930s. He described the behaviours of different leaders, identifying three different kinds of leaders:

- Autocratic
- Democratic
- Laissez-faire

Lewin claimed that autocratic leaders made decisions solely on their own interpretation of what needed to be done quickly. They made no reference to any other opinions. Lewin recognized different degrees of democratic leaders: some were more democratic than others. Unless the need for a decision was particularly pressing, these leaders allowed input from colleagues, often weighing up the worth of others' opinions before making a final decision. Lewin's interpretation of a laissez-faire leader was one who guided a team of colleagues but sat back and let them make their own decisions. This type of leader would be best described as a motivator or facilitator in modern terminology.

Contingency Theories

Failure to come to any firm conclusion regarding the personal characteristics of leaders led to the development of theories that focused on the situations surrounding the leader. One of the more popular theories belonging to this category was the Hersey-Blanchard Situational Leadership Theory. Basically, this involves the mental capacity and maturity of the leadership team. This theory was developed by Dr Paul Hersey in 'The Situational Leader', and by Ken Blanchard in 'The One-Minute Manager'.

According to Hersey and Blanchard, a good leader alters his style of leadership in accordance with the person being instructed. There is little point in giving instruction in language so far above the head of the person you are instructing that they are unable to understand what you are talking about. The idea of giving instruction is to delegate a job and get it done, not to prove that you are so far above your subordinate that they can see that they cannot possible compete.

This Situational Leadership theory displays four styles of leadership:
- Telling (instruct subordinates with significant detail)
- Selling (gain cooperation from subordinates)
- Participating (consult subordinates before finalizing the decision)
- Delegating (set goals for subordinates but leave the details to them)

Put simply, the first two styles involve making sure the job gets done. The last two involve empowering another person to have the skills to do the job. A leader who exhibits participating and delegating skills is leading more through facilitating than through simply instructing. There are loose similarities between autocratic leadership and the 'telling' style of leadership; 'selling' leadership has various indications that might mimic democratic leadership; 'participating' and 'delegating' both appear similar to the laissez-faire leadership style.

This leadership style includes related ideas on the maturity levels of the subordinates. Charismatic leaders adapt their styles of leadership according to the "maturity" of the person being led. The maturity levels have four divisions from M1, the lowest, to M4 at the most mature level:
- M1: Not skilful enough or not responsible enough for the task; or not willing to do it; work is not always consistent in clarity, precision and effectiveness
- M2: Willing to do the task, but unable to take full responsibility for it; coherence, relevance and efficiency of communication are not always present
- M3: Willing and able to do the task, but lacking the confidence to take responsibility; however, maintains a secure and discriminating acquaintance with the field of leadership
- M4: Experienced, skilled, willing, and confident in taking the task and responsibility; evidence of insight, intelligence and effectiveness in relation to the work in hand

When leading somebody with an M1 level of maturity the leader should use the 'Telling' style. When leading somebody with M2 level of maturity, or somebody whose skills are limited, the leader should employ the 'Selling or coaching' level of leadership. For the M3 maturity level which often tends to include somebody whose skill levels are quite high but who tends to lack confidence, the leader should recognize the style of leadership required is the 'Participating and supporting' role. The highest maturity level or M4 should be matched with the 'Delegating' level of leadership. Overall, what Hersey and Blanchard are saying is that it is up to the skill of the leader to recognize which kind of leadership needs to be used in which situation.

Power and Influence Theories, including Transactional Leadership

These theories move away from leading from the front to guiding at the side, using power and influence to get the tasks done. Probably the best known of the Power and Influence Theories is that referred to as French and Raven's Five Forms of Power. As its name suggests, this theory consists of 5 arms:

- Legitimate: "Do as I order since I am the CEO"
- Reward: "Do what I suggest, and you will be rewarded"
- Coercive: "Do what I order, or else you will suffer the consequences"
- Expert: "Do what I suggest, since you know that I am the expert in this field"
- Referent: "Do what I suggest, since you respect me as a person and role model"

Referent leadership may involve charismatic charm or celebrity status. It is especially potent when combined with any of the other forms of power. This can include '*leading by example*' or '*walking the talk*' as highly effective ways to establish a positive leadership influence. This can be destroyed when the leader behaves contrary to the message. Such behaviour is a betrayal of the workforce and will entail the loss of referent power for leadership.

A good leader can get people to do things they do not necessarily want to do, by inspiring them to follow where the leader goes and by creating a vision for others. The strength of that vision and the encouragement from a charismatic leader are often enough to inspire others to follow where they lead. A charismatic leader is committed to share their vision with others and then use the strength of their characters to make that vision happen.

Transactional leadership is a form of leading by influencing through structured rewards. The United Kingdom's National Health System uses Transactional Leadership by rewarding each individual step up the ladder with slightly higher pay. This is a task and reward system that works very efficiently, gets the job done and gives the staff an incentive to achieve the next level.

More Recent Leadership Studies

Two buzzwords from the 1970s and 1980s on leadership qualities were "vision" and "transformational leadership". Studies during the 1980s tried to establish the importance of leaders attempting to ensure their subordinates recognized the organizational vision. At the same time the differentiation between leaders and managers emerged, described as '*transformers and transactors*' by Burns in 1978.

In 1985 Bennis and Nanus wrote that "*Managers are people who do things right and leaders are people who do the right thing*". They also said that "*Management controls, arranges, does things right; leadership unleashes energy, sets the vision so we do the right thing*". The base line is that anybody who has the task of supervising subordinate personnel needs to be both a manager and a leader. Furthermore, leaders help to shape the policies of an organization whilst managers carry out that vision; but the managers also need to carry some of that vision with them as well.

According to DePree, "*the first responsibility of a leader is to define reality*" [p. 9]. To define reality is to set the organization's vision. Manasse established four criteria for vision within organizations:

- Organization

- Future
- Personal
- Strategic

Organizational vision provides a snapshot of how the <u>organization</u> will look in the <u>future</u>. <u>Personal</u> dreams and ideals drive individuals for their own ambitions. <u>Strategic</u> vision unites the other three groups, connecting their reality so that vision can be translated into action [Manasse, 1986: 162].

Three leadership categories emerge from this concern for organizational vision:
- Shared Vision
- Valuing Human Resources
- Transformational Leadership

Shared Vision

Unless efficient leaders share their vision for appropriate action with their teams, that vision cannot possibly materialize. A good leader delegates vision so that thought becomes word and deed. In Luke 10:1, Jesus appointed 72 disciples on 36 small missions: an excellent example of delegating authority and leveraging resources. Also the disciples internalized the vision by sharing in the work, rather than continuing to simply listen to Jesus and watch Him do the work.

If a leader shares the vision but finds that those insights were not put into practice, then that leader is ineffective or complacent. The management team is responsible for achieving the leader's vision, and must take responsibility if they fail to achieve it.

Vision becomes activity only when shared and the directions are followed. Again, look at the story in Luke 10: 1-17. Jesus shared gave specific instructions to the 72 disciples, and they successfully performed as required.

Valuing Human Resources

Positive relationships should develop as the result of leaders sharing their vision with the rest of the organizations they operate in. These positive relationships encourage the kind of environment that leads to effective contributions from other individuals within an organization, heartened by the support of an efficient and effectual leader. Skills are ascertained and expanded as a result of individuals becoming encouraged to contribute to challenges posed by supporting a team effort, in cases where a leader has empowered teams to carry out leadership's shared vision for changes in policy that will benefit the organization in the future. In other words, this fulfils the concept of transformational leadership, described by Burns as: "...*leaders and followers raise one another to higher levels of morality and motivation*".

Transformational Leadership

Transformational leadership changes people and social systems; ideally "transforming" followers into leaders by helping them internalize the organization's ideals and goals.

Perhaps if today's leaders had followed Burns' interpretation of transformational leadership, the financial chaos of the past few years could have been minimized, if not avoided all together. In fact, putting today's global recession into the concept of transformational leadership as opposed to transactional leadership could well put the whole saga into context. A number of studies can be attributed to the definition of transformational leadership in terms of 'fulfilling a common purpose' and 'developing commitment in respect of leaders to, and with, their followers'.

Compare transformational leadership with Burns' definition of transactional leadership: "leaders who motivated by appealing to followers' self-interest". The result could easily be a portrayal of leaders such as Alan Greenspan and the effect his leadership had on the collapse of the US economy. Talking about transactional leadership, Bass interprets this form of leadership as 'appealing to strong emotions' in their followers but not necessarily attributing this to 'positive moral values'. Leadership that exhibits such irresponsibility can be interpreted as being both dysfunctional and complacent and, with hindsight, can be applied to the situation that developed with the leadership of the US Federal Reserve.

Leaders responsible for the US economy were given adequate warning that maintaining interest rates at an artificially low level was asking for trouble. Since 2002 leaders in the US economy were advised to regulate the banks. While corporate government became complacent, the selling of toxic assets began to have a detrimental effect that would see Lehman Brothers collapse and rock the assets of Fannie Mae and Freddie Mac to the core. The resulting downturn in the US economy reverberated around the world, bringing other financial institutions with it.

Characteristics of Leaders of Change

There have been a lot of studies on styles of leadership and the differences between leaders and followers. However, regardless of theoretical research, what is critical to every organization is effective and efficient leadership. Leaders need to be able to motivate their team of managers to carry out their vision of policy changes. The most recent studies on what makes an effective leader have attributed this characteristic to sharing their vision with others and in collaborating with their human resources to put this vision into practice. It is only a short step from being an effective and efficient leader to being a dynamic leader that is able to inspire and encourage change within an organization.

Communicators and Listeners

This is essential for any leaders of change: communicating and listening skills are essential characteristics for leaders. They must develop, articulate, share and sell their vision. At the same time, leaders must demonstrate that they value the contributions from their management team and other subordinates. To be a leader of change it is essential to be able to communicate effectively and to be able to listen, as well as to quickly weigh up any risks and take responsibility for whatever outcome arises.

Leaders of Change are Proactive

Leaders of change recognize the need for their organization to change. They are prepared to take the initiative and predict when those changes need to be implemented. Mazzarella and Grundy explain a leader's attitude to the need for change, "*...always testing the limits in an effort to change things that no one else believes can be changed*".

Or as Pejza said a "*leader continuously scans the environment noticing where change is needed*".

Nevertheless, two things leaders of change have in common is their proactive ability to respond to conditions that require changes and to recognize that change is necessary before it becomes essential. This allows sufficient time for an appropriate change management plan to be put into effect, rather than leaving the need for change so late that it all has to be done in a hurry. Proactive leaders of change tend to be people for whom traditions, rules and regulations are not stumbling blocks to a recognized need for change.

Effective leaders of change are sensitive to alterations within their environment and are able to recognize the need to respond to these swings. As DeGues said, "*Understanding the changes occurring in the external environment and then adapting beliefs and behaviour to be compatible with those changes*".

Leaders of change "*access the reality of the present and determine the gaps that exist*", said Joiner.

In a nutshell, an effective and proactive leader of change needs to be a prudent risk taker.

Leaders of Change are Risk Takers

An effective leader of change will recognize opportunities that will improve an organization, as Joiner noted: "*Change must be initiated by leaders who are willing to risk their reputations for the future benefit of their companies*".

Leaders of change have the ability to encourage change to happen. An effective leader of change always worked '*for the identification of the most appropriate procedure through which change could be secured*' as Becker wrote. Few leaders of change are willing to "*live within the constraints of the bureaucracy; they frequently violated the chain of command, seeking relief for their problems from whatever sources that were potentially useful*".

Nickse summed up the characteristics leaders of change needed to exhibit: "*believe totally in your goal, have all the data, stick to your topic, study each aspect without flinching and then charge ahead*". Successful leaders do not take risks indiscriminately; they take careful thought as to the consequences.

Summary: the Characteristics of Effective Leaders

Two essential characteristics for effective leadership have been recognized as:

- **Initiating structure**: concern for how the organization is run
- **Consideration**: interpersonal relationships between colleagues and how this can be encouraged

Other characteristics that are important in a leader of change include:
- Being visionary
- Valuing human resources
- Effective communication and proactive listening
- Taking risks

The art of communicating and listening can be linked directly to the characteristic of consideration that values the interpersonal relationship between colleagues and recognizes and encourages an organization's human resources. This has been more than adequately summed up by Joiner: *"Effective change requires skilled leadership that can integrate the soft human elements with hard business actions"*.

After this chapter's emphasis on "leadership", the next chapter turns to "management" theories, as exemplified by some of the best and most effective.

Chapter 4 – A REVIEW OF MANAGEMENT THEORIES

Like the overview of "leadership", this review of management theories will provide the basis for understanding the "Corporate Turnaround" approach to reviving an ailing company. Specifically, this chapter explains how the notion of "management" developed over time...and why mere "business management" fails to address the leadership required for corporate change.

'Management' is a pretty new field. There is little to be found that is much older than a hundred years. Yet entire libraries can be filled with management books. This vast explosion is simple to explain: prior to the 1850s, businesses were mainly family affairs, and small in scope. Some large organizations existed, but these were almost exclusively in the hands of nations (army, tax collection, public works) or the institutional Catholic Church, and all were focused on 'administration' in the sense of what we now call 'bureaucracy': uniform rules to keep things together.

The key point is that management's goal was to maintain the status quo, not to lead corporate change. Management generally had little to do with stimulating growth, turnover or profits. One could rightly argue that taxes were perhaps a different affair, as they often did focus on squeezing the maximum out of mostly poor people.

The only notable exception to national or religious organizations, of which I am aware, is the Dutch East Indian Company. This was the famous 'VOC' – and to a lesser extent its British counterpart – which was indeed the first worldwide operating-for-profit private company. It was indeed huge. For almost two hundred years, from 1602-1800, it dominated world trade. With nearly 5,000 ships and almost a million 'expats', it was indeed the first in many respects: the first MNC (multinational company), the first to issue shares, and the first private company ever to grow so big. But again, their whole organization system was focused on meticulous bookkeeping and administration, and not on 'management'. Maybe that is the reason that, when it was dissolved in 1600, after years of decline, its acronym VOC had become widely known as '*Vergaan Onder Corruptie*' – Perished By Corruption. Personal interests had totally undermined the interests of the company. Something we would attribute today to 'bad management'.

It is only with the advent of the Industrial Revolution that larger companies came into existence. The process of mechanization did not only stimulate growth, but also the need for capital. As a lot of capital was needed, a larger group of 'investors' had to join together, who became of course particularly interested in profits and returns. As the 'work' was outsourced to other people, control systems were put in place. Some 'methods' could be copied from history, such as controlling large armies. But with the change in focus, a different approach was needed. But – besides a lot of internal disagreements, particularly when the Board was composed of non-related individuals – the whole system of management was a very 'personal' affair of the captains of industry.

Let's take a quick dash through 150 years of history, condensing the stories of three notable leaders and then seeing whether modern theory has finally grasped the essence leadership. These leaders are:
- Frederick Taylor

- Max Weber
- Elton Mayo

This chapter will then contrast "management" with "leadership".

Frederick Taylor against the Captains of Industry

One of the first to realize this, analyse it, and put into a solid framework, was Frederick Taylor (1856-1915). By the turn of the century he challenged these captains of industry that their 'rule-of-thumb' style of management would systematically underperform against Taylor's proposed new system of 'scientific management', applied by a group of 'ordinary men'. He certainly was a genius in breaking complex tasks down into smaller subtasks and even still smaller sub-subtasks – something that is still rule number one in systems management – and then applying a 'scientific' way in optimizing each of these smallest parts.

Although he was later often criticized to have 'dehumanized' labour activity, that his methods lead to make workers into imitations of machines, I am not so sure this is all correct. Human working conditions before Taylor were certainly not better. Just think about the British coal and steel industry in the 19th century.

From an economic point of view, Taylor's scientific management became a worldwide success. Productivity improvements of 200% to 300% were regularly achieved applying Taylor's methods. And standardizing repetitive tasks (e.g. assembly lines) worked well. Breaking larger tasks into smaller tasks and assigning workers to execute these smaller tasks in small units of repetitive movements, made it also easier for them increase output speed, learn faster, and earn higher rewards.

Max Weber and Henri Fayol – Bureaucratic Management

Following the success of Taylor's ideas in scientific management, Max Weber (1864-1920) extended the same idea into the administrative part of the company. Although his main field was sociology – he saw society moving from a 'value oriented' to a 'technocratic oriented' way of thinking – he applied his and Taylor's ideas to develop a set of principles that would lead to an 'ideal bureaucracy'. Again the core element was to break down complex tasks in a series of simple steps, controlled by a rigid top-down hierarchy of management and subordinates.

This system was no doubt embraced by the British and applied in their former colonies, where much of it is still very visible. Cashing a check in a bank in Sri Lanka typically involves at least 3 or 4 levels of filling in a form, checking and approving multiple times, where the check and the form(s) go up the hierarchy and (sometimes much) later coming down. Be prepared that the whole process takes at least half an hour, while in a bank in Western Europe, the same is done by a single clerk in 2 minutes or less.

Where Weber was more of an observer than a designer, Fayol's theories on administration take Weber's ideas to a next and much more detailed level. Starting from defining the principal roles of management as commanding, coordinating and controlling, Fayol – being himself a successful manager – focused more on the practical side of management. His five roles, the three mentioned above being preceded by planning and organizing, are still widely in use today.

Elton Mayo and the Human Relations Movement

It all started with Elton Mayo's Hawthorne Works Experiments in the early 1920s. With the mechanizing and dehumanizing effects of Taylor's and Weber's ideas as they were applied in various industries, reactions of unions put pressure on government regulations to give more prominence to the individual character of workers and employees. With a slowly growing importance of the HRM (Human Resource Management) departments, and under the influence of the behavioural sciences, emphasis was shifted from a purely organization-centralized view for efficiency and productivity, to finding a balance between the needs of an organization and those of the workers. Starting with the effect of lighting on worker productivity, the Hawthorne Works Experiments evolved into a whole series of experiments on the effects of various working conditions: rest breaks; free or charged meals; variations in working hours; and so on.

These experiments challenged the Taylor/Weber principles. They underlined the importance of growing from a set of individuals to a group or team; they showed the importance of variation in work methods (in direct opposition with Taylor's standardization of repeating always the same) to avoid boredom; and the positive effects of freedom (against the strict hierarchical control). Group dynamics, teamwork and participation entered into the scene, stimulating greater trust and openness in the working environment.
While all four of the above giants have still much to say in 'modern' management, management itself – as all things – has evolved in integrating, extending and refining the described ideas. In fact, their ideas have grown so much into our society as 'common sense', that it is often difficult to believe that at those times these were new and revolutionary ideas.

Modern Theories

Of course it did not stop there. The last thirty years have seen an unending series of 'new' theories and principles. Each professor in Management added a few ideas, gave it a slightly different name – driven or not to earn a place in the Hall of Fame – and the shelves on Management Literature in university and company libraries kept growing. A few of the headlines perhaps: Contingency Theory ('it all depends'), Systems Theory (input, process, output) and Chaos Theory (events are rarely controlled). In the 70s there was a regular hype about 'a systems approach'. Anything that looked a bit 'logical' received the label 'a systems approach'. At that time, if you wanted to boost sales, just adding 'a systems approach' as subtitle, would have the book sell like hot dogs.

From Management to Leadership

One of the consequences of the Human Behaviour Movement has certainly been the growing distinction between Management and Leadership. Where Management concentrated on the more 'technical' aspects, e.g. all kinds of quantitative methods, including forecasting, operations research, production management, etc., Leadership became the human focal point: how to work with people, how to motivate people, how to recruit the best people, etc.

This has sometimes gone to the point where you could be a good manager, but a mediocre leader, and vice versa. In Biblical terms this internal conflict is also exemplified by the personality conflict between the two sisters Martha, who was busy with the material things, and Mary who focused on people [Luke 10:38-42]. In business terms however, I do not believe in this distinction. A bad leader will be a bad manager, despite solid technical and analytical skills.

Unfortunately, where most Business Schools excel and compete on the basis of excellent management education, I have not seen any shine in leadership. Perhaps this is because leadership is not so easy to master, or to teach. There is still the general belief that you are born as a leader, or not. Now that is also wrong. Leadership is definitely a question of learning, but more of the training kind. While you can learn a lot of management techniques out of a book, with a few exercises to get the feeling, leadership does not come so easily. It is first and foremost training an attitude, learning to listen, and developing skills of empathy, with touches of psychology and other disciplines. Likewise, it is also a matter of maturity. Hence, you see a lot more on leadership training in executive MBA programs than in regular curricula for traditional students at the undergraduate level.

Material on leadership also tends to be a lot more fragmented. While books deal mainly in 'leadership theories', many of the more fine-tuned techniques – the 'real' stuff – are found in published articles. Better than yet another definition, a recent list of worthwhile articles perhaps serves best to give a 'feeling' of what leadership is all about[5]:

New Paradigm in Management (including in Leadership)
WoT's Hot and WoT's Not: Leadership in the Next Millennium
'Do As I Say, Not As I Do' Doesn't Cut It Any More
Don't Wait to See Blood
A Burning Commitment to Our Cause
A Coach's Playbook for Leaders
Sunrise Interrupted: Leadership & Choice-making
Beyond Manipulating and Motivating to Leading and Inspiring
Leaders Care for Organization Culture and Context
Leaders Give People Space to Grow
Leaders Help People See Beyond What Is to What Could Be
Leaders Invest in Growing and Developing People
A Tale of Two Managers: Command versus Commitment
Building Passion and Commitment the Wal-Mart Way
Growing the Leader in Us
Tough Times Call for Strong Leaders
Leadership: How Important Is 'Integrity'? In Today's Business World Is Integrity an Afterthought?
Five Benefits Of Leadership Development Coaching

Do you see the difference as compared to a Management book's table of contents?

Leadership in a Changing World

In the context of global economies and a fast paced changing world, the qualities of leaders are

---

[5] Dr. Carter McNamara, Free Management Library
http://www.managementhelp.org/ldrship/ldrship.htm

often becoming more important than perfect management. There are no sure answers anymore. Our world has become as fuzzy as the atomic structure. Gone are the solid particle electrons of Rutherford and Bohr. The future is in the hands of quantum mechanics, incorporating Heisenberg's Uncertainty Principle. Even the world of business has become a world of probabilities.

Has managing change has turned into the practice of magic? Will "business management" be considered an art, rather than a science?

Indeed, companies and organizations are faced with changes like never before. The West is in decline, the NYSE is tumbling, but the sun shines in the East: London and New York are passé; India and China are the new places to be. Steel production, the stronghold of the old economy in Europe and the US has moved into Indian hands. The largest American steel producer, U.S. Steel is on the 10th place in the world list (2008), with the numbers 1 to 9 all in the East (attributing ArcelorMittal to India, even if the HQ is still in Luxemburg). Toyota, Honda, Mazda and Nissan have pushed aside Ford and GM. The Customer Service Centre that answers your inquiry or complaint is located in Bangalore, Hyderabad or Delhi. Your clothes and shoes are coming from the Philippines, Vietnam, Bangladesh and Sri Lanka. Software is cracked in Pakistan and on the market in Hong Kong even before it is officially released in the US. The best ranked MBA programs are still offered in the old world, but already 6 out of 30 are in the East and moving up fast, according to the Financial Times ranking in 2010[6]. And the ranking criteria of alumni salaries, is at least controversial.[7]

It is the 21st century version of 'To Tell the Truth': will the real Leader please stand up? And will we know where to look to see this Leader? How will we recognize one who does arise?

After the tour of historic captains of industry, the next chapter views some of the modern issues with crisis management. In these cases, no clear solution has been found, so the outcome is still in question; no leaders have emerged with the answers.

---

[6]FT.com website: Global MBA Rankings 2010
http://rankings.ft.com/businessschoolrankings/global-mba-rankings
[7] Salaries in Asia are much lower than in the US. This pushes down the ranking of Asian institutes in the global list, since most of their alumni are working in Asia at a lower salary than they would earn when working in the US.

Chapter 5 – MANAGEMENT AND CRISIS MANAGEMENT

It is one thing to manage a company that has already achieved a measure of success. It is another to manage a crisis. Several corporations are listed as examples of how complacency with past achievements can become crippled, unable to change because of their entrenched management structures or business practices.

Can a leader "think outside the box" of a corporate structure or a society's mindset?

Overview

In order for a business to survive during tough times there needs to be a strategy for coping. A good leader who can carry an organization through a period of crisis needs to be able to facilitate an emergency management strategy in response to crisis management to ensure the healthy continuity of the organization. For every organization to survive in uncertain times it is necessary for them to develop a strategic response to risk in the form of Corporate Governance. For this to be successful there needs to be an integral crisis leadership team to call upon when the situation requires it. Planning in this way for inevitable problems in the corporate world results in an organization's superiority over those lesser commercial concerns that failed to plan for strategic survival. In other words, the resilience of an organization can be measured in their degree of disaster avoidance as a result of the strength of their crisis leadership.

Crisis Leadership and Crisis Management

Crisis leadership is the ability to provide effective executive leadership under pressure enabling organizations to survive in a changing environment. Through suitable crisis management it is possible to convert crises and threats into opportunities to be savoured. This takes action but in order to take action it is necessary to face unpalatable facts, rather than maintain an organizational denial. It is a fact of life that it is far more comfortable to deny a problem exists that to root out the problem and eliminate it. After all, that may involve intruding on allegiances. You may have to withdraw your support from the executives who are responsible for boardroom decisions. This is hardly likely to be a comfortable decision, no matter how obvious the personal failings of an organization's boss might be to those around him.

There is a psychological precedent, revealed in a study by Professor Jeffrey Nutter from the University of Georgia, USA. His evidence revealed that denial is so much more comfortable, in a psychological sense, than facing up and admitting to problems. Evidence of this can be seen with the recent change in British politics. New administrations tend to blame previous problems on failures in their predecessors, yet the results of those failures are still in evidence. It takes a new government to sweep away the old entrenched ideas in order to be able to move forward effectively. In other words, these failures of the old leaders are translated into action by the incomers. Even so, it has already been voiced amongst the media: how long before this new administration begins to fall into the same traps that befell the previous government?

WICH Management Structure

Perhaps I am being cynical here, but the WICH strategy is alive and well, and deeply entrenched in much of British management, from BA and their treatment of the unions to the NHS and their deeply divisive management structures that alienate the medical and nursing profession who attempt to carry out the jobs they are trained to do, often in direct opposition of the management who should be supporting them. Basically WICH – or, 'Who's in Charge Here' operates by division and acrimony. It results in recriminations and resentments but seems to be uppermost in many of the large organizations that are centrally funded by Whitehall.

The benefit to the overall leaders of each department is that they know where the opposition is, and where the threat to their power lies. It flourishes amidst incremental pay bands based on time served as much as qualifications gained. It does not necessarily mean the best person for the job is selected, however. The best of the WICH strategy eventually leads to incompetence and confusion, with so many quangos being commissioned yet none being answerable to any one source. British Rail, when it was an amalgamated structure worked, if not totally efficiently. At least it achieved what it was set up to do: run a network of trains around Great Britain.

Then, along came privatization and British Rail was split up into Rail Track plus a host of individual companies that provide the rolling stock and another host that actually run the trains: the network has become so divisible as to be ineffective, inefficient and unprofitable. This has led to loss of public confidence and resulted in an election that has produced the first hung parliament for over 30 years. Let us hope the new coalition between Conservatives and Lib Dem does not evolve into DNDW: Do Nothing…Delegate….Watch!

How Conflict can Reshape Companies

Modern markets are changing how organizations have to adapt, completely integrating the concept of change management into the whole management concept itself. This is calling for a new style of manager in each department as the whole organization has to change from within each individual department to have any chance of being able to affect the organization at the top. However, for the new style of management to move forward the old management style of compartmentalization, set into a hierarchical mould can no longer function. The new model to take organization forward into the modern age of uncertainty involved integration amongst the departments, and a move away from the basic concept of R & D being the source of new product ideas. New ideas were sought from outside sources and integrators and facilitators took the place of individual departmental heads. Tightly knit teams of specialists worked together to achieve the result of a project allocated to them and for which their team was solely responsible.

Crisis and the Leader
Despite previous recessions, the recent financial crash took many of the world's leaders by surprise – or, rather, they had a rude awakening. This recession did not happen overnight and it certainly did not happen in isolation. Perhaps it may be too strong a criticism to state that many of the world's leaders were in denial, but many did not consider it prudent to acknowledge the signs, which, to onlookers, were becoming clearer before the financial crisis was upon us. Leaders had no plans in place to manage the crisis and, the more they attempted to improvise in the wake of unfolding events, the worse the situation became. In hindsight, the signs were all there if anybody cared to look. Unfortunately politicians and regulators were both in denial that events could escalate out of control.

Greed, profligacy, extravagance: they all mean much the same when the outcome resulted in the collapse of Wall Street. Again, we are talking about denial amongst the leadership, perhaps mixed with complacency at all levels of management leading to a culture of leadership that became dysfunctional through its denial – turning a blind eye towards any irregularities such as the fact the banks needed to be regulated, despite warnings. Nevertheless, the US economy was booming as a result of interest rates being kept artificially low. Credit rating agencies also contributed towards the incipient disaster that was waiting to unfold.

At the same time, collateral debt commitments were accruing. If the credit rating agencies had been operating effectively instead of turning a blind eye, these debts would have been downgraded to toxic assets. They should have been downgraded to toxic assets; they were not. Credit rating agencies may have allowed the accruing toxic debts to slip through the net but the financial expertise at the GSAs, Fannie Mae and Freddie Mac as well as those at Lehman Brothers should have recognized these collateral debt commitments as being toxic assets, with a potential threat for financial disaster. It was common knowledge to the directors within the financial sector that the two GSAs were contributing as much as 50% towards the USA's debt during 2002.

It should not have come as too much of a surprise that there was going to be a major fall-out to the housing market at some not-too-distant date in the future. Alan Greenspan, who headed the US Federal Reserve during 2004, has to take considerable responsibility for the eventual fall-out since he opposed tougher legislation for regulating the financial derivatives, coming down in favour of the adjustable-rate mortgages for the ordinary house purchaser, backing the sub-prime mortgage market to the hilt.

The 80/20 Principle

It is easy to put this in the jargon commonly used today: time management and just-in-time marketing. Basically the 80/20 Principle refers to the philosophy of Vilfredo Pareto. Despite his death being nearly nine decades ago, his ideas have been kept alive and are the subject of books by Richard Koch and Nicholas Brealey, amongst others. Pareto's Law involves identifying which tasks take how much time or cost to complete. Typically 20% of the tasks take 80% of the time or cost to complete. Then identify which 20% of tasks provide 80% of the benefit in production units or sales dollars, you will note that they are usually exactly the same. Therefore, the remaining 80% of the work only gains 20% of the benefits. Imagine that: 80% of both time and cost is being allocated to garnering just 20% of the results in any organization. In an ideal world you should be able to eliminate the "80% effort" tasks to achieve a more cost-effective organization. The other trick is to determine how to do more of the "80% result" tasks.

Psychology of Business

Our brains are constructed as neural pathways. Some of these pathways have been designed to draw out specific, surprising information from areas of ordinariness. This principle is often referred to as 'sensitization of attention'. The human brain has been programmed to pick out information that might be hidden from immediate view and, once we have picked out something that has drawn our attention we then seek to establish patterns using that information. In just the same way insects are attracted to brightly colored flowers, so our brains pick out certain signals: a readiness to perceive that leads to rapid recognition. Psychologists refer to this phenomenon as sub-threshold activation. In other words, we receive input from the world around us. Specialist clusters of neurons then receive this input, which are all made ready to react in response to stimuli. This concept is the basis for the CoRT (**Co**gnitive **R**esearch **T**rust) program and the business model that has been labelled the DATT (**D**irect **At**tention **T**hinking) Thinking Program. CoRT Thinking focuses different aspects of thinking into three basic principles:

- Thinking is a skill that can be developed
- The perception stage is where the majority of thinking is carried out
- Thinking needs to be taught. The best way of teaching is through the tools method.

Meanwhile, the DATT Thinking concept involves learning how to use the Direct Attention Thinking Tools that have evolved as a result of the CoRT Program. Basically, without getting too technical these tools, once learned, can cause your brain to work at a more efficient level because it has been trained to react in a certain way to specific stimuli. As an example of how this method of brain training can be relevant to business, one of the training courses being offered is the Lateral Thinking course which teaches you how to develop your innovative perceptions and think creatively. In turn, if you incorporate these new ways of thinking into existing business models you are likely to achieve effective results.

Maximum Exertion of Powers

Is this superior strategy mentality necessary to achieve full potential? This has been called many things in many different quarters. The Bible often refers to the mind of the believer. Philippians 2:5 "Let this mind be in you, which was also in Christ Jesus". In 2 Timothy 1:7, "God has not given us the spirit of fear; but of power, and of love, and of a sound mind". Is this constant striving necessary? This striving can be interpreted as attempting to reveal superior powers and greater capabilities than the next person. It is how these powers are applied, however, that makes the difference. There have been many large corporations that have risen, phoenix-like from near annihilation by the sheer power applied by their leaders: companies such as Komatsu, for instance. In a way, Komatsu's leaders can be judged on what they have achieved which can be translated back to the character of those leaders.

When it comes to Kingdom principles, we are judged on our character first and foremost. We are judged on the state of our hearts and minds. If our hearts fulfil the high standards expected of leaders within the Kingdom of God then the good behaviour exhibited as a result will culminate in good leadership being revealed. In both Titus 1 and 1 Timothy 3, Paul requires a leader to be "blameless...sober (and) just". James 3 advises every person to learn to control his or her "tongue", intending that we be careful about what we say so as not to give offense.

This chapter moved from crisis management and leadership avoidance, through the psychology of business and into an introduction to a Christian view of leadership. The next chapter examines a number of "business cases" from the Bible: several great leaders whose faith and deeds in the Old Testament can serve as inspiring examples today. That chapter will also note some non-Jewish leaders who came later in history, but whose leadership styles are also instructive.

Chapter 6 – LEADERSHIP AND CRISIS

If traditional "common sense" management fails to resolve an organization's crisis, there can be only two outcomes. Either the crisis destroys that organization, or a radical leader succeeds by applying new solutions.

In times of crisis traditional management fails and innovative leadership emerges. This seems to be a pattern that repeats itself throughout history. Whether an upcoming crisis is the alarm sign of weak leadership, as is often observed during the decline of a civilization, or a sudden crisis such as a natural disaster creating havoc under existing management, it is invariably a time where a 'strong leader' emerges, takes over, and leads the community out of the crisis into a new future.

John P. Kotter paraphrased this in 2001: "*Most U.S. corporations today are over-managed and underled*" [8]. There is often too much management and not enough leadership. Clearly, management is much better defined, easier 'to learn', and can be quite effective in times of relative peace. But when things get rough, it becomes a different story.
It is certainly no coincidence that most of great leaders have climbed the stage in times of great difficulty. You do not manage a crisis, you survive it. The 'normal' management rules do not apply anymore, and people, including the 'managers', feel they are standing on shaky ground. They often panic and lose control. That is when 'leaders' pop up, sometimes out of the sky, uniting the 'people' with a common vision – how to solve the problem - and empowering them to really do it.

Abraham and Moses

One of the oldest examples in history is Abraham, leading his people out of Mesopotamia to Canaan, about 4000 years ago. The story is told from Genesis 12 onwards. The reasons for leaving are not very clear. Finding a better place to develop their monotheistic religion, away from the pagan society in Ur or Haran is just one element. Possibly Ur was invaded regularly from the north. However the vision for a better future is strong: "*Go to the land that I will show you. And I will make of you a great nation, and I will bless you and make your name great.*" [Gen 12:1-2]. This was the vision of the Promised Land. With his little clan he made it across Mesopotamia. For some odd reason, they passed all the way through Palestine and, two generations later his grandson Jacob ends up Egypt.
Abraham also brought a new element in the tradition: hospitality. Against the common belief that hospitality was written with a capital H, this was not the case in that time. Travellers were more likely to be robbed, murdered and raped than treated with respect. But Abraham made it differently: One day, in Mamre, he saw three men passing. "*When he saw them, he ran from the entrance of his tent to meet them* "[Gen 18:2]. He gave them water and food, and when they left, he even went with them (in the direction of Sodom) to put them on the right track. This habit of hospitality and 'going the extra mile' has ever since become a typical attitude, adopted by later generations, and still very much a living tradition in Muslim culture throughout the Middle East.
Some 700 years later, the next great leader, Moses, will finish the trip. Here the 'crisis' is very serious: enslaved in Egypt, hit by famine and plagues, it was the worst of times for people of

---

[8]John P. Kotter, *What Leaders Really Do*, Harvard Business Review 2001
http://hbr.org/2001/12/what-leaders-really-do/ar/1

Israel. With the same vision and devotion as Abraham, Moses leads his people to a better future, returning to Palestine. Now, Moses is a special case. He became the leader somewhat against his own will. Raised in the royal court of the Pharaoh, he was culturally probably far from his Hebrew brethren. They saw him as an Egyptian, rather than a son of Israel.[9] But after killing an Egyptian while defending a Hebrew who was being beaten, he realized he had lost his royal status. Not an easy position to hold: to the Hebrews he was an Egyptian; but to the Egyptians he was a Hebrew.

While he had to escape the influence of the Egyptian court, he hid in Midian. Most people do not know that Midian is a region around the northern edges of the Red Sea, where later on the exodus out of Egypt would pass again. There Abraham had passed on his way to Egypt. It was there that Moses most likely connected with the Hebrew tradition, working in the service of the priest Jethro. In the first encounter with Jethro's daughters, he was definitely still viewed as an Egyptian.[10] But, after marrying one of Jethro's daughters, he was pretty much settled down in Midian, when he received his mission on the neighbouring mount Horeb: *"I have come down to deliver them from the hand of the Egyptians and to bring them up from that land to a land that is both good and spacious, to a land flowing with milk and honey, to the region of the Canaanites, Hittites, Amorites, Perizzites, Hivites, and Jebusites. ... So now go, and I will send you to Pharaoh to bring my people, the Israelites, out of Egypt."* [Ex 3:8-10].

So, back he went, and the rest is known: Moses received a bit of help from above in letting loose the (in)famous 10 plagues on Egypt, before the Pharaoh consented to releasing the Israelites. With half a million people Moses returned through the desert, probably the same route he had already taken two times before, to the land of Canaan. Of course, travelling with such a large group of people makes things a bit more difficult, and more time consuming.

A peculiar thing about Moses was his extreme humility and shyness, and on top of that he had a speech problem; likely he stuttered. These are not the characteristics one would expect from a leader. *"The man Moses was very humble, more so than any man on the face of the earth".* [Num 12:3]. *"I am not an eloquent man ... for I am slow of speech and slow of tongue".* [Ex 4:10].

So what made him stand out above the crowd, and even above other leaders? It is his attitude of servitude, born out of his humility. Among all other leaders and prophets, he acted from the bottom of his heart, wholly dedicated to God, in the consciousness that everything he had and did was not his, but came from God: *"If there is a prophet among you, I the Lord will make myself know to him in a vision; I will speak with him in a dream. My servant Moses is not like this. (...) With him I will speak face to face, openly, and not in riddles; and he will see the form of the Lord."* [Num 12:6-8].

Consequently, the power of his leadership came radiating from his face: in him, people could see the face of God, directly. In this, Moses was unique and equalled by none, except Jesus.

Non-Biblical leaders

A similar pattern can also be seen in other, non-Biblical, leaders. Genghis Khan, although widely known for extreme cruelty, also brought such a new element to Mongolian culture. He not only

---

[9]Ex 2:14 *"Who made you a ruler and a judge over us?"* the fighting Hebrews replied to Moses.
[10]Ex 2:19 *"An Egyptian man rescued us from the shepherds".*

expanded the Khan Empire to connect the Caspian Sea to the Chinese Sea, bringing relative unity among the people of Central Asia, he also introduced a common script, and, contrary to the prevailing tradition, introduced a compensation system based on merit and loyalty, rather than family ties. In the same way, when conquering new lands, he did not kill or chase away the enemy soldiers, but took the conquered tribe under his protection, and even integrated its people into his own tribe. In later years, this gentleness was not always applied in a consistent way, particularly when capturing cities, but during the early years, it certainly helped the fast expansion of the Mongol empire.

If another human being ever equalled the type of leadership such as that of Moses, the closest I can come up with is Mohandas Gandhi. His humility was legendary. For a lawyer, he was clumsy in public speech. But anyone who he met could feel his deep love for India and his respect for even the most humble human being. His greatness came out of his smallness. Peace, love and truth, all three in boundless quantities, were the core values of his strength and leadership. His everlasting reach for peace was personified in his way of 'Satyagraha' or passive resistance. His boundless love and respect for India and its people was perhaps most visibly exemplified in him wearing a *dhoti*, a symbol of homespun clothing. ('Swadeshi' is making use of local or indigenous products). His uncompromising search for truth and honesty meant he would never ask people to do what he would not personally be willing to do himself. These characteristics make him to the finest leader of the 20th century.

He was truly a man of the masses, showing the extreme power of passive resistance. He personified the Indian 'man-of-the-street', to which he gave all his respect and love. His ways inspired other leaders around the world.

Defining great leadership

Being a great leader does not mean that you can always bring home the anticipated or expected results. Gandhi failed to get the British salt tax removed, even if his salt march in 1915 was probably one of his greatest achievements. The tax was only abolished in 1946! Neither was he successful in keeping India unified. He failed to overcome the mistrust between Hindus and Muslims, and seeing the country split into two states (India and Pakistan) was, on a personal level, probably his biggest failure.

Neither does it mean that a leader is good. Adolf Hitler is a notorious example of this. His leadership was vicious. Once he came to power, the Nazi party took full control over the country, and every aspect of civilian life. Installing the Gestapo and the SS, gave him the necessary tools for eliminating all opposition, without being questioned. But he inspired the German people, fortified the economy and made Germany rise again after the disastrous effects of the First World War. He was a visionary. The country, which had been in shambles for more than twenty years, became strong again. Germany had built a full network of 'Autobahn' highways, at a time when Route 66 (America's first highway-to-be) was still mostly dirt road. Much like Genghis Khan, Stalin and other dictators, he ruled with an iron fist. He was ruthless, but brought prosperity and hope. Even if he now personifies cruelty and evil, much of that only became public after WW II was over. The way he showed determination and perseverance, and the way he could inspire people and move them into action, does made him a great leader; although it was the wrong kind of leadership.

This brings us back to the beginning of this chapter, to John P. Kotter's distinction between management, focused on order, and leadership, focused on change:[11]

Managers	Leaders
Plan & budget	Set direction
Organize & staff	Align constituencies
Control & solve problems	Motivate & inspire
↓	↓
Create order	**Produce change**

In one word: a leader makes change happen.

To elaborate a bit on Kotter's views, setting direction involves a critical analysis of the present. Hard and challenging questions must be asked, and alternative answers evaluated. It is here that a new vision is created and consequently a new strategy needs to be developed. This is the most fundamental step in deviating from a management perspective, which is essentially devoted to creating order and eliminating risk in the present situation. This is almost the opposite of what is needed to open a new direction. Hence, often heavy objection can be expected from a traditional management, as all the 'old values' risk to be torn apart. Of course, although risk is inherent, a new direction should be taken carefully. Not all can be done at once; research will be necessary; as well as a lot of meetings. So this is a phase that takes time. The 'leader' will need to take it one step at a time, defining a broad direction first, which will be refined over a number of revision cycles.

In the second step, alignment, it is all about communication and relations. It is meant to bring the different views in line with each other, and with the broader vision of the company, organization or nation. It is the search for a common ground and a common strategy that must be crystal clear to everyone involved. If everybody is not pulling the same cart, and in the same direction, the whole will never reach its destiny. This is most likely the most difficult of all tasks, as the managers and leaders involved will need to be brought on the same road ahead, all while being convinced that this is the right way to go. Here 'true' leadership will come out at its best, on the one hand inspirational and convincing, and on the other hand open for questioning and willing to change the original plans.

Once everyone is indeed 'aligned' to the new vision, and a broad strategy has been defined, the bulk of the work is still ahead. Now leadership will gradually become more 'inspiring', giving the example, and passing on energy to complete the tasks and make things happen. Gradually, leadership will involve more 'management', creating order in the chaos, and bring down the strategy in attainable tactics. With the broad vision laid out, it is easier to follow the path, but the amount of work involved asks for persistence and endurance. And there is a lot of energy going into that. It is similar to a presidential election campaign: once the elections are won, it takes four or six year of endurance to 'make it happen', which is, after all, the hardest part. And particularly in a business environment, it will take time – a lot of time – to see the results of the new vision and strategy. Getting there is a task for giants. Keeping motivation high, particularly

[11] J.P. Kotter 'Leadership Facilitator's Guide' preview, p. 8
http://www.enterprisemedia.com/misc/leadershipkotterprev.pdf

in times of pressure, it is not easy. Reflect on Moses' trip from Egypt to Canaan. How many times did the caravan halt, needing a new injection of 'energy': fresh water at Marah; manna from the skies; and the Ten Commandments? After a while, morale sunk again, and needed to be renewed. It is a miracle that they finally reached their destination.

And it is also a task that no single person can bear. Jethro advised Moses, his son-in-law, to sub-divide the task of judging the Israelites. Leadership must be shared and distributed. Leaders are needed in several places, on several levels. So leadership must be nurtured and developed among a larger number of persons involved. Making the right pick in the first place can prove decisive for the end result. Often this involves nominating people with potential on places or in roles they are new and not always ready for. They will of course be excited at first, but will need a lot of support, motivation, and possibly training, to give them the endurance and perseverance they need to bring it to an end. It is in this phase that Genghis Khan proved to be successful, whereas Hitler failed. Hitler surrounded himself with technically capable people, but there was only place for one 'Fuhrer', controlling everything and everyone. Genghis Khan however succeeded in his endeavour to create a massive empire by selecting, mostly, the right people and giving them 'real' power. His successor did not do so well, and the empire shrunk quickly in the years after Genghis Khan. The empire had lost its unity, and fell into pieces, with its leaders competing among themselves.
Although Moses had a set of good inspirational leaders for each of the tribes, he often found similar resistance and disagreement among them. We'll see some of this in the coming chapters. But at least he managed to keep the flock together until the borders of the Jordan River, within sight of the Promised Land.

Having reviewed a few leaders in some depth, next we will take a broader survey of Biblical leadership: ten people whose faith or pride led them on fascinating journeys. Again, it will be up to the readers to discern how they fit into the management patterns as demonstrated by these Biblical leaders.

Change Management Leadership – A Biblical Perspective

The world has come a full circle
We've begun a new economic cycle
The sky is stormy and the seas rough
The going is no longer easy but tough

The time to change is upon us
The time to rearrange is a must
How can you know what must we do
It is easier than you think, it is inside of you

Chorus
The good book has been written and shows us how
The good book is needed, needed right now
So learn your scriptures and apply them to your firm
Only like this will we ever prosper and start to learn

For the three-phase plan is the way out
Have faith in the plan and have no doubt
For surgery, resuscitation, and nursing
Will make companies rise and sing

King David and Joshua show us how surgery
Transformed kingdoms and did what was necessary
To make the world as they wanted it
To make the world as they believed in it

Chorus
The good book has been written and shows us how
The good book is needed, needed right now
So learn your scriptures and apply them to your firm
Only like this will we ever begin and start to learn

King Solomon and Apostle Paul with their diplomatic ways
Show us that this can be the way that pays
As markets enlarge and resuscitate
Brings a better world and a brighter fate

Nursing brings us hope and much inspiration
Moses and Abraham spawned many imitations
Great leaders have benefited all of humanity
Great leaders have inspired great humility

Chorus
The good book has been written and shows us how
The good book is needed, needed right now
So learn your scriptures and apply them to your firm
Only like this will we ever begin and start to learn

Jesus Christ is the ultimate change manager
Unafraid to challenge despite the danger
He used the three phase plan to resurrect
Important values and beliefs, to guide intellect

He used surgery to get inside, get to the core
Of the soul of the world and resuscitated it pure
His nursing techniques touched many men and hearts
And when his end came, Christianity did start

Chapter 7 – LEARNING LEADERSHIP THROUGH FAITH

You could call this chapter a transition chapter. Stepping away from the leadership theory, our focus is redirected to another source of leadership, the Bible, presenting ten short biographies. These are ten biblical personalities, who, somewhere in their lives, became leaders. You will follow the process of how simple men turned out to be great leaders. Ten short introductory case studies, which, hopefully, will help you how to develop your leadership qualities and apply it in today's corporate environment. This initial overview will be further deepened in the following chapters of this book.

David: Surviving Adversity and Success with Humility
[Dawood in the Islamic tradition]

If you're looking for a 'small' and 'simple' character, a figure like David easily comes to mind. As the youngest of eight (brothers), the way he was chosen by God through Samuel for a higher purpose is a real Cinderella story [1 Sam 16:1-13]. Shortly after that, he received his first assignment to the court of King Saul, playing the harp. Otherwise, as youngest in the family, he was herding his father's sheep. By accident, again, he visited the battlefield between the Israelites and Philistines, to bring food to some of his brothers who were serving in the army; it 'just happened' to be the right moment when Goliath was defying the Israelites. Now, everybody knows the story of David and Goliath [1 Sam 17], glorified in art and stories throughout history. How the little guy, David who symbolized Israel, defeated the giant Goliath who represented the gentile world. A touching story indeed because of its 'dimensions', but was it really a miracle? No, not at all! Let's face it: from the beginning, Goliath did not stand a chance. Neither sword nor spear can ever defeat a sling or a bow. Close combat is just of a different order. This was not a fair fight. The real story goes beyond this.
That all were shivering of fear is quite understandable seeing the size of Goliath. The strangest of things however is how David spoke directly with King Saul, and convinced him to let David take it up with Goliath. After all, the faith and future of all of Israel was in the game. To me, Saul's decision to put Israel's future in the hands of little David is the core of the story. First, Saul dared to see beyond the obvious: the battle-hardened giant against the youth. Second, Saul analysed the 'real' situation: Goliath with all his weaponry was much less mobile than David simply carrying a sling and a few stones. Finally, Saul had the courage to let David fight in his 'usual' outfit, proven to have worked in the past against lions and bears. (David could hardly walk when wearing Saul's armour; remember that Saul stood "head and shoulders" above other Israelites). While it says nothing about David's leadership abilities, it says everything about Saul's.

So, for David's role in this chapter, we have to look further. After the 'heroic' fight with Goliath, David gets a regular place in Israel's army, and performs well. Of course, marrying one of Saul's daughters, Michal, was a jump-start. But as army commander he became very popular. In fact, he performed so well that Saul became jealous of him, and tries to eliminate him several times. But each time, David grew more popular with the people. At the end the pressure becomes too much for both, and David had to flee into the Philistine territory. After Saul's death, David became king of Judah, and later, after the death of Saul's son Ish-Boshet, also king of Israel. He has unified the whole country, brought lasting peace, and created order into a previously tribal society. He had quite the success story. His fame as warrior, ruler and lover is almost unequalled in the Bible. His wisdom radiates and vibrates through all the Psalms (many of which are attributed to him, but are not written by him). He also moved the capital to Jerusalem, as shown by housing the Ark of the Covenant there. A master of survival and certainly one of the most charismatic leaders in the whole book, David had his flaws too. His popularity with women was legendary, but he did not escape God's wrath: his adulterous relationship with Bathsheba brought a series of catastrophic events including rape and murder among his own family and children. But after all, it is a great and vivid story, spread out over most of 1 and 2 Samuel. Coupled to the eternal image created by Michelangelo's David, who would not be charmed by this outstanding personality?*

Elisha's Self-Sacrificing Spirit
[Also Elisa, Eliseus or, in the Islamic tradition, Al-Yasa]

Elisha was the disciple of Elijah, from whom he 'inherited' the role of being the leading prophet of Israel, after Elijah was taken up into heaven. It all began while he was ploughing the fields – the humblest of tasks, just as David was herding sheep – and Elijah called him. He followed. No questions asked, no conditions requested, apart from informing his parents and family, he just took his things and followed, humbly and with courage. For about twelve years he followed Elijah on all his trips, a period which passed in utter silence – at least in the Bible – until the moment Elijah was taken up into the heaven by a fiery chariot, just over the Jordan River, close to Jericho. And even then, after twelve years, he only made a most simple request: bless me with 'a double part of your spirit' [2 Kings 2:9][12].

From there onwards he exhibited an impressive series of miracles and healings, starting right in Jericho. Typical for Elisha is that his miracles are not always of the life-saving kind, but often 'little' blessings, which make life more comfortable, much in the style of Jesus at the wedding in Canaan. To save a widow from a creditor, who wanted to enslave her children as repayment, he multiplied the little oil she had into a quantity sufficient to repay the creditor, and enough to provide for her family [2 Kings 4:1-7]. This was followed by blessing a rich woman, giving her a son – and later resurrecting him from early death – out of thankfulness for her great hospitality [2 Kings 4:8-37]. Much of the remainder of the book 2 Kings is a continuous story of the many wonders, predictions and miracles of Elisha, which includes a number of prophesies about battles and wars.

Gideon and the 300

Gideon was a simple farmer, the youngest member of the clan that was the weakest in their tribe. His story is found in Judges 6 and 7.

Gideon's first feat demonstrated his blend of courage and caution: he replaced an altar to Ba'al with one to the God of Abraham; but he did this at night, because his neighbours would be angry. Indeed, when they did discover who vandalized the altar, he escaped death only thanks to his father's support.

Gideon also famed for "putting out a fleece". He thought God had told him to fight against the

---

[12] Note: in biblical terms, 'a double part' actually meant the 'first-born rights'. When a man died, and left 3 sons behind, his belongings were divided into 4 parts: two parts for the first-born son and one part for each other son. So the request was in no way 'greedy', but just confirming their close relationship: let me be your eldest son.

Midianite raiding parties. To be sure that God had instructed him, he placed a sheep's fleece on the ground, asking that it be wet with dew while the grass would stay dry. After finding it so, he then asked God to reverse the test. The next morning, the fleece was dry whereas the grass was wet.

Gideon is best known for winnowing his army from 32,000 down to 300 before the big battle. First the fearful were sent home, leaving 10,000 combatants. The second test was to drink from a river. Those who knelt to drink were disqualified; only the 300 who scooped up water in their hands passed the test.

This story shows that a leader needs to select followers carefully. Choose the willing, rather than coercing those who would otherwise quit. Trust the prudent; a soldier on his knees, with his face in a river, is far more vulnerable than one drinking from his palms.

Why were these characteristics so important for Gideon's followers? Their battle tactic was to sneak into the enemy camp at night, with torches concealed inside pottery jars. After infiltrating the camp, Gideon's troops smashed the jars and blew trumpets. The sudden light and noise frightened the Midianite raiding party: many killed each other as they fled into the night. Gideon's "army" needed stealth, courage, patience and alertness to carry out the plan. Therefore Gideon had to choose only "the best of the best". The leader, Gideon, selected a highly skilled "management cadre" for this task.

Often preachers overlook the final three verses of Judges 7. Once the Midianites had fled, Gideon called for reinforcements from several tribes who engaged their enemies over a significant expanse of Israelite territory. The leadership lesson here is to use "followers" when appropriate.

Moses and Crisis Management

God had just drowned the Egyptian soldiers as they pursued their escaped slaves. The Israelites rejoiced. Then, in Exodus 15:22 through 17:7, they entered the desert of Shur. After three days without water, they found an oasis named Marah; but the water was too bitter to drink.

The story does not say whether Moses was concerned before "the people grumbled". However, he did respond quickly to their complaints. He called out to God, who told Moses how to make the water fit to drink.

Chapter 16 sees the caravan on the move again; this time there was no food for the people. Moses heard the complaints, and God again instructed Moses. This time, Moses had to pass along the rules for gathering manna. Although some people did not follow the instructions correctly, eventually this became the staple food for the Israelites through their forty years in the wilderness.

At the start of chapter 17, they found another dry area near Rephidim. The pattern was repeated: the people grumbled, Moses checked with God, and then the problem was resolved.

I do not remember any sermons questioning Moses' leadership, but perhaps he should have anticipated that hardships would lead to complaints. Perhaps he did, but had reasons for avoiding taking pre-emptive action. A modern preacher might say that God wanted the Israelites to learn to be patient and endure hardship without complaint.

Modern leaders would prefer to avoid crisis situations by planning carefully and executing those plans flawlessly. Since real life does happen, leaders must also be ready to act when things go wrong and customer complaints flood into the office.

Moses is an exemplary leader in the field of crisis management. He hears the complaints, determines the correct response, and takes the appropriate action quickly, decisively and effectively.

Noah, a Man of Action

Genesis 6:8 begins the story of Noah, the man famous for building the first boat. The main story has three phases. First, God told Noah of the coming flood, and instructed him to build the ark as the way to preserve his family and some animals. Noah built the ark. Then God told Noah to put the animals, and the food, into the ark; he did. Once the floods had receded and the land had dried, God told Noah to "abandon ship" to repopulate the earth; again Noah did so, in Genesis 8. Noah took decisive and timely action. Undoubtedly his neighbours mocked him for building the ship. No one believed in the disaster for which Noah was preparing.

Nebuchadnezzar's Pride and Failure

Nebuchadnezzar was king of Babylon. He had a disturbing dream, which only Daniel, one of the exiled Israelites, could interpret. This dream predicted that King Nebuchadnezzar would become insane, would live like a wild animal for some time, and later would return to sanity and power. One year later, Nebuchadnezzar bragged about his palace, his city, and his own power and glory. At that time, his sanity left and the dream came true. Sometime later, after his hair and nails had grown long and unkempt, he raised his eyes to heaven, and praised the God who had such power over him.
Recent history has shown many leaders to have "feet of clay", although that phrase relates to another Babylonian king. People may fall from popular favour without falling victim to mental illness.
Sometimes the first misstep is to boast. Nebuchadnezzar was especially boastful in appropriating all the credit for "his" achievements, in Daniel 4:30. He has forgotten that the city of Babylon had been built centuries earlier, and that others had done the physical work required for his architectural triumphs.

Joab: the Right Place for Glory

Joab was King David's field general. David had delegated a routine siege of an Ammonite city, Rabbah, to Joab in 2 Samuel 11:1. While David remained in Jerusalem, he became involved with Bathsheeba. When most of that affair was resolved, Joab sent word to David that the city of Rabbah was ready to be taken. "Now muster the rest of the army…and capture the city. Otherwise I will take the city, and it will be named after me". (2 Samuel 12: 28 [New International Version 2010]).
David's earlier problems with King Saul are told elsewhere in this book. Part of the trouble was that the Israelites were praising David above Saul. "Saul has slain thousands, but David tens of thousands". King Saul did not share his glory easily.
Joab did not make the same mistake. He had spent at least nine months in the field, besieging Rabbah. Once he took the water supply, their days were numbered. Whoever led the final charge would be credited with the victory. Joab did not want to take that glory away from his king.
A wise leader shares the praise and rewards for success with others. Doing so increases loyalty, trust and co-operation. Appropriating accolades will lead to the opposite results, and perhaps active betrayal.

Jeremiah Does the Right Thing for the Business

Jeremiah 32 is the story a business transaction under unusual circumstances. The prophet Jeremiah was imprisoned for telling Zedekiah, king of Judah, that Nebuchadnezzar of Babylon would win his war against the Israelites. Jeremiah was a traitor, advocating accommodating the inevitable victor.

According to Jewish law and custom, land should be sold to the nearest relative rather than to a stranger. Jeremiah's cousin offered him a field in the neighbouring territory of Benjamin…an area certain to be conquered along with Judah, if Jeremiah's predictions were correct.

Yet Jeremiah agreed to buy this field. The transaction is painstakingly described, including the way that a copy of the documents would be sealed and stored.

On the surface, it seems Jeremiah threw away 17 shekels of silver. Perhaps these seven ounces or 200 grams would have represented a significant portion of Jeremiah's retirement fund. One may suspect that Jeremiah's cousin Hanamel actually believed Jeremiah's doom and gloom predictions. Hanamel liquidated his family's assets, perhaps to flee the country before he became a victim of war.

Nonetheless, Jeremiah was sure God had told him that He would bring Israelites back from Babylon, restoring their prosperity and improving property values.

Leaders must take into account both current conditions and long-term trends. Leaders must be prepared to invest for future growth, even while taking cost-saving measures in the near term.

Samuel: from Humble Beginnings to Success

The early Israelites practiced polygamy. Elkanah had two wives, but Hannah was the one who had no children. She felt disgraced and unfulfilled despite Eli's love. One of the times when she prayed, Eli the priest saw her and said "May God grant your desire". Elkanah and Hannah soon had their son, Samuel. But Hannah gave him back to God by arranging for him to serve in Shiloh where Eli was the priest.

Eli's two sons were already adults, serving as priests although they did not honour the traditions or follow the letter of the laws regarding the sacrifices. Samuel, as a small boy, would have had menial tasks. Until the night God first spoke to Samuel, no one would have paid attention to the small boy working for the priests. Samuel's career prospects were very limited, because the priesthood was a hereditary position. Eli's sons were already "in the business", and the story hints that they had heirs before they died.

Sometime after Eli and his sons died, Samuel rallied the Israelites. He gave spiritual guidance, encouraged his people in defending their borders, and served as a circuit judge, hearing cases and dispensing justice. Later, against his own counsel but under God's guidance, Samuel anointed Saul as the first king, and David as the second.

Modern leaders may find themselves in a position to take charge when the need arises. The first necessity is to be present, faithfully doing the jobs available. The second key attribute is the ability to take charge when circumstances warrant.

Paul's Quest for the Truth

Saul, as he was known among his colleagues the Pharisees, approved the persecution of Christians: the Jews who believed that the one God had a divine Son who came back from death.

In fact, Saul asked the high priest for the job of rounding up any of Jesus' disciples who may have gone to Damascus to hide from the persecution in Jerusalem.

While riding to Damascus, Saul had a vision of Jesus. He converted and became even more zealous as a Christian missionary, church planter, teacher and writer.

Saul had been raised in Tarsus, a Roman city. With his background and Roman citizenship, he became the "apostle to the Gentiles". At that time, most Christians were ethnic Jews who may have considered themselves as part of a progressive movement in Judaism.

Saul began using his Roman name, Paul. On one missionary journey, he visited Athens, the seat of knowledge in the Mediterranean world. Acts 17 reports on his debate with Athenian philosophers and scholars.

Many of Paul's letters show his flair for sophisticated logical arguments. His quest for truth made him a feared persecutor of Christians, and then their most famous early apologist.

Leaders must seek truth and follow it where it leads. Telling people what they want to believe may make a sale, but ultimately leads to a downfall.

Now that the readers are thoroughly steeped in theories and examples of leadership, it is time to explain "Corporate Turnaround". This three-phase technique for rescuing a distressed company requires knowledge and skill; but also a different type of leadership must be expressed in each phase. The next chapter introduces "Corporate Turnaround".

Chapter 8 – The "Corporate Turnaround" Model for Change

Where is Your Company Heading?

If you are leading a business organization that runs smoothly with high profits, excellent cash flow, contented shareholders, eager employees and satisfied customers, then you are to be highly congratulated.

Unfortunately that state of affairs might not last forever. Many businesses are reeling from recent economic crises. Some major financial institutions fell when property-based securities became toxic waste. Several major automobile manufacturers required billions of dollars in government bailouts. The American recovery is moving at a snail's pace in the early months of 2011. Countries with strong economies would prefer to see interest rates rise, as insurance against inflation that would erode their current strengths.

Or perhaps your organization needs strong leadership, aware that it is in dire straits already.

It is not enough to have a competent manager who can "do more of the same". A company in trouble needs to turn around and go in a new direction.

Who sets the direction? The strong leader, who must manage change, and not simply manage the company, sets the direction.

Corporate Turnaround: The Map for the Journey

How does this leader know what direction to take? Perhaps a wise person could figure it out, given enough time and reference material. But the company is in a crisis **now**, and cannot wait for trial and error experiments.

The "Corporate Turnaround" model is the map for this journey. This model has been used with great success in a number of companies. It charts the path for organizational change.

What kind of person can serve as a leader for this radical process of change management? Several leaders, many from the Bible, will serve as role models.

Introduction to the "Corporate Turnaround" Model for Change

The three-phase "Corporate Turnaround" model has been used in dozens of companies in North America, Europe and Asia. The "Corporate Turnaround" method has been proven to make your business revive, live and thrive.

"Corporate Turnaround" uses the image of treating an ill patient. You, the corporate leader, have the role of the doctor in charge of this patient. What methods are appropriate? What kind of leadership style is required? What actions must be performed to save your patient...your business?

Even the most desperately ill companies can benefit from applying all three principles of corporate turnaround. Even the healthiest might benefit by using the "Nursing" phase. The "in-between" companies, with slow growth or a declining customer base, or challenges in retaining staff, should find these resources helpful.

The three phases of "Corporate Turnaround" are:
- Surgery
- Resuscitation
- Nursing

The next chapters provide more detail, but here are the highlights.

Surgery Phase: To Cut is to Cure

Surgery is a drastic medical treatment. The surgeon removes a diseased part of the body in order to cure the patient.

Corporate Turnaround prescribes surgical techniques as the first steps in promoting health in a corporation. If the company is bleeding money, then the first treatment is to cut expenses. Re-structuring is the typical task. The goal is to improve cash flow and prevent insolvency.

This step does require leadership and finesse, not just a penchant for making people miserable. However, the leader must be resolute, able to decide quickly and to insist on action and results. The goal is to increase productivity by eliminating wasteful expenses and concentrating on the core business.

Joshua is a Biblical character who had displayed the leadership required for taking drastic measures.

Resuscitation Phase

The medical analogy is to provide post-operation treatment. After surgery, the patient will be weak; the treatment begins with assessing the patient's condition and determining his or her current capabilities.

This phase concentrates on developing new business in a strategic and focussed manner. It is necessary to set realistic objectives, open new markets, and then move swiftly to improve cash flow. Something like the Roman god Janus whose two faces look backward and forward, the leader in the resuscitation phase must continue working for immediate results, while also planning for future growth. The primary task is to make sales and cross the break-even line from loss to profit. The secondary task is to develop new opportunities.

A Biblical character who had displayed this kind of second-stage leadership was King David.

Nursing Phase

This phase provides therapy for the patient. A physiotherapist or occupational therapist becomes involved at this stage, training the patient to strengthen weakened muscles or to learn how to adapt after the traumatic surgery.

The corporate patient must develop new internal strategies and learn to work in new ways. One example is the development of an improved corporate culture. The company must find a balance among an aggressive push for sales growth, the on-going pursuit of efficiencies, the development of new capabilities or products, and a steady rise in quality. As well, the leader must foster new attitudes within the organization; a new acceptance and pursuit of making on-going changes for improvement. The company is then ready to pursue sustainable long-term growth.

A Biblical character who had displayed this kind of leadership was Paul, the apostle to the Gentiles.

For ease of reference, each phase of the "Corporate Turnaround" strategy will be presented in its own chapter.

Chapter 9 – Phase One: SURGERY: The Autocratic Leader

A Company in Need of Surgery

The Corporate Turnaround methodology prescribes surgical techniques as the first steps in promoting health in a corporation. If the company is bleeding money, then the first treatment is to cut expenses.

Change Management Leadership for the Surgery Phase

This step does require leadership and finesse, not just a willingness to make people miserable. The goal is to increase productivity by eliminating wasteful expenses and concentrating on the core business. This also sets the stage for future growth and profitability.

Internal and External Causes of Corporate Disease

Some corporate diseases develop due to internal problems. These include:
- Poor management: Too timid or too bold; either acting without planning or procrastinating endlessly
- Ineffective financial controls: failure to audit; slow pursuit of receivables; weak budgets
- Operational weakness: poor logistics; lack of competitive sourcing; weak marketing
- Low morale: insufficient training; lack of meaningful employee recognition
- Failed projects: lack of cost control; too dependent on highly-leveraged takeovers

The key point for internal problems is that your company can indeed make changes.

Other corporate diseases may be blamed on external causes, such as:
- Changes in government regulations
- Changes in consumer tastes
- Economic conditions, such as a global recession
- Currency fluctuations
- Sudden appearance of low-cost competitors or cheaper technological alternatives
- Natural disasters, wars, terrorism, or national uprisings

While some of these external problems may appear "out of the blue", two factors are important:
1. The organization should have contingency plans
2. The company can take steps to remedy the situation for itself, if not for the country

The Steps of Surgery

The following steps are used during the "surgery" phase of corporate turnaround:
- Communicate

- Concentrate
- Control Costs
- Control Cash Flow

Communicate

Communication is one key. The CEO must start by forming a team to guide the corporate turnaround. If the CEO can communicate clearly to this team, then the team can assist by communicating with their staff members.

This enlists more participants, and grows the support for the turnaround. The CEO needs to communicate with a clear, no-nonsense, take-charge style. This builds confidence in the rank and file; it also decreases the amount of discussion and pushback that could otherwise slow down the turnaround project.

Concentrate

The company in distress has few resources, which must be concentrated on a few key tasks. This is the time to cut losses by selling unprofitable divisions and to focus on the core business. Sometimes, even a marginally profitable sideline must be terminated in order to keep the main company alive.

Control Costs

Everyone talks about cost control, but few actually succeed. Zero-based budgeting forces every manager to justify each expense. Cutting the operating budget requires sacrifices, starting with executive perks such as business-class flights and accommodations.

Since downsizing the workforce leads to long-term morale problems, a turnaround CEO should examine other opportunities. Will staff accept a wage cut, whether in pay-per-hour or in a reduction in hours?

Downsizing should begin in the executive suite. Can the management pyramid be flattened to achieve significant cost savings?

Reducing fixed overhead or asking suppliers for competitive bids might achieve other cost savings.

Control Cash Flow

As noted above, short-term cash flow can improve dramatically by selling an underperforming division of the company. Even some profitable companies improved their books by selling and then leasing back their office space.

Right sourcing is a term that is replacing "off-shoring" and "out-sourcing". Determine the right place for a task to be performed. In many cases, teams from other countries with lower wage scales can perform standardized intellectual work. This usually has a cost in convenience and communication: someone may need to make telephone calls at unusual times, and cannot simply walk over to someone's desk to look over a document.

Another approach to improving cash flow is to stretch payables and compress receivables; the latter is usually preferable since your supplier may punish your company with penalties or delayed shipments of goods. It may be necessary to take drastic steps with your customers: improve the credit checks before finalizing a sale; sue for payment; or sell older receivables to a broker who specializes in this work.

Joshua, an Autocratic Leader

Joshua had one of the worst starts possible for a CEO.

He first appeared in Exodus, helping Moses lead the Israelites after their escape from Egypt. Joshua and Caleb were the only two (of twelve) spies who gave a positive report: "We can conquer the Promised Land". The other ten convinced everyone that the mission was impossible, leading to forty years of wandering through the wilderness. So Joshua's first recommendation was rejected by popular "vote".

Moses had been a very hands-on leader. His father-in-law had to convince Moses to hire extra judges, because it was too much work for Moses to handle all the disputes. Moses had spent forty years speaking to the Israelites on behalf of God. In addition, Moses had been the leader in several military campaigns, winning some land east of the river Jordan.

Joshua had big sandals to fill. He had to rally the Israelites to follow him and put their confidence in his leadership.

The first project was to cross the Jordan River, the barrier that Moses had been forbidden to breach. This was an early test of Joshua's leadership: several tribes had already been permitted to take land on the east side of the Jordan, but were supposed to send their soldiers west to help take the rest of Canaan. Would they comply? Or would they reject Joshua's authority?

Joshua reminded them of the pledge they had made to Moses. The reply was "Whatever you command, we will do...just as we fully obeyed Moses, we will obey you". Joshua passed this first test of leadership.

The battle for Jericho was an example of Joshua's autocratic leader. "March around the city once today, and every day for six days. On day seven, march seven times and then attack". This was quite a test of discipline for the priests and soldiers, to hold an ineffective parade outside the city they were besieging. But the results were amazing, when the walls fell on the seventh day.

For the attack on the village of Ai, Joshua gave very clear military orders. He told 30,000 soldiers to wait in ambush, while he attacked the village with only 5,000. The soldiers followed his instructions, the ambush succeeded, and they were victorious.

Most of the book about Joshua tells of his military leadership, but Joshua 17 speaks more to his political abilities. One Israelite "tribe" had descended from Joseph (famous for his "coat of many colours"). They complained to Joshua that they had been allotted too little land for their "numerous" tribe. Joshua replied that they were free to roust more Canaanites out of a forested region. After all, "you are numerous and very powerful…you can drive them out".

One of the final tests of Joshua's leadership mirrored the first. Having conquered enough land west of the Jordan, he sent the soldiers who were to settle the east bank back to their families. But those people built a new altar to God, one that was not approved by Joshua or the other Israelites. This nearly started a civil war; it was seen as an act of independence and rebellion. Rather than sending his army, however, Joshua sent a delegation to learn why this had been done. When told that the purpose was to mirror the official altar as a reminder of the real one, Joshua's delegation was satisfied and called off any military response.

Joshua followed the "steps for surgery":
- He communicated clearly, instructing his army with precision and clarity
- He concentrated on conquering one city at a time
- Joshua's "cost control" was focussed on minimizing the loss of troops: most of the battles were routs
- Joshua's "cash flow" was measured by the spoils of war: aside from the city of Jericho, which was essentially sacrificed to God, the Israelites were enriched by the cattle they took from every city they conquered

Chapter 10 – Phase Two: RESUSCITATION: The Democratic Leader

Resuscitating Your Company through Short-Term Projects

At this point, the company needs to begin its transition to full health. The medical analogy is to provide post-operation treatment. After surgery, the patient will be weak; the treatment begins with assessing the patient's condition and determining his or her current capabilities.

Change Management Leadership for the Resuscitation Phase

While this phase also needs decisive action, Resuscitation requires team building. It begins to develop a greater depth of leadership and also starts transforming the organization into one that can adapt to future changes.

Primary Steps in the Resuscitation Phase

This phase concentrates on developing new business in a strategic and focussed manner. It is necessary to set realistic objectives, open new markets, and then move swiftly to improve cash flow.

The seven major steps are:
1. Determine corporate objectives
2. Keep it real
3. Develop the right product at the right price
4. Implement an aggressive marketing strategy
5. Differentiate using service quality
6. Strengthen the brand name
7. Invest in future expansion

Let's examine these in greater detail.

Determine Corporate Objectives

Many distressed companies suffer from poor vision. Specifically, they cannot see their objectives, and therefore flounder aimlessly. Perhaps a better illustration is that of a rower who has lost sight of land. Even the strongest efforts will not dock the boat, since the rowing is aimless.

So the CEO must settle questions such as:
• What is our corporate mission?

- What are our products and services?
- What are our key distinctive features?
- What gives us a competitive advantage?

In a turnaround situation, there is not much time for soul-searching and quiet reflection. Many of these questions may already be addressed in company slogans or in corporate minutes. Yet too often the company has not used those answers to determine what products, price points, or quality standards it should implement.

Keep it Real

External consultants can give valuable perspective at this stage, to determine what really is happening "on the ground". Yet the CEO must be personally involved to get a feel for the issues.

Political reasons may make hiring external "therapists" more palatable. They are paid to give advice; they do not need to toady to the leader for a promotion; and they do not have a vested interest in one part of the business over another.

External consultants will be expensive, and more so if they are given complete responsibility for assessing the corporate situation. The usual recommendation is to supplement an executive task force with carefully selected external consultants.

Develop the Right Product at the Right Price

Product leadership is an important long-term goal for any company. Avoid jumping on a bandwagon being steered by your competitors. Engage with your customers, learn what they desire, develop that product and then market it in ways that trigger their attention and their response.

Pricing is an interesting problem, because it is intertwined with cultural values. For example:
- A white middle-class male might compare three low-cost products and decide that the most expensive is likely to perform the best
- An Asian mother, reviewing the same products, could suggest that the lowest price meets her criteria: "cheap and good"

Sometimes the novelty of a product drives the price. When first introduced, contact lenses were built and sold to last a fairly long time, with a high price to match. Disposable contact lenses are much cheaper, or else customers would not dispose of them; but would customers have had confidence in cheap disposable lenses in the first years that expensive long-term lenses first became available? Perhaps they needed to become commonplace before they were acceptable at a low price.

Implement an Aggressive Marketing Strategy
This process is a bit like performing CPR to restart a patient's heart: pump hard to keep the blood, or cash from sales, flowing.

Retain your best sales teams, even if you have to cut staffing in other areas. Without sales, your company cannot survive.

If you have not developed a web site or expanded into e-commerce or social marketing, now is the time to push for these sales channels. To keep costs under control:

- Learn from someone with experience in developing such a sales channel
- Consider starting an online "boutique" that offers a limited selection of products (for example, all available from one warehouse, with common shipping costs), rather than trying to sell all your products from everywhere to everyone. Larger projects will cost much more than smaller, as more exceptions will be found

Pricing, sales events, advertising, contests, and give-aways: many types of medicine are available for the patient during this phase.

Differentiate using Service Quality

Product and price are important, but so is the quality of the product that your customers think they are buying, and the quality of the service delivering and supporting that product.

As an example, North Americans "enjoy" a vast network of fast-food chain restaurants. Some outlets gain more customer loyalty by remembering individual clients than for the obvious differentiators such as location, price or type of food. This kind of service is difficult for the restaurant chain to manage or even encourage; but the local franchise can use it to advantage.

A Japanese cultural tradition says "the customer is God". This leads to no-holds-barred efforts to resolve any customer complaint quickly and conscientiously.

A long-term view would be to start a quality assurance program to measure, control and improve the service experience for customers.

Strengthen the Brand Name

Whether is the company's name, the product name, a logo or other design element, your "brand name" is vital for marketing and sales. Which fast-food restaurant chain did you think of, a few paragraphs ago? That company has succeeded in imbedding their "brand" into your mind and memory.

When people buy products, they are exchanging their known cash (or credit position) for an unknown. They hope that the product is not defective and will serve their needs; but there is always an element of doubt. The stronger your brand, the more credible is your promise that their money is well spent.

Invest in Future Expansion

This is the final step in the Resuscitation phase. Once the previous measures have begun, the CEO should cast about for future business opportunities for the company.

Many reasons are given for a "Merger and Acquisition" (M&A) strategy for expansion:
- Cost savings through consolidation of basic functions
- Global outreach, including a "one-stop shopping experience" for other global enterprises
- Access to an innovative product or service

Unfortunately, there are even more reasons why M&A projects fail to deliver shareholder value in the long term. When investing in a foreign market, for example, one might assume that one citizen equals one consumer. In China, however, many internationally available products are too expensive for a significant percentage of the population. Your company may be pursuing a saturated market. The CEO might approve a deal simply because of the ego boost; the signing bonus may sweeten the deal, but is secondary to the prestige of making the acquisition. Companies with more money than muscle often try to buy success by buying a successful start-up firm; if they do not have the endurance to continue working at the marketing and product development, they will simply have spent some money. Finally, expanding requires money: to hire experts to assist with due diligence; to pay for bonus or severance packages; to cover delayed receivables and larger inventories; and for the inevitable I.T. consolidation projects.

Regardless, some M&A expansion projects do succeed.

Other examples of investing in future expansion are:
- Capital investment in new production equipment, whether to increase capacity, for operating efficiency, or to improve product quality'
- Purchase of licensing of intellectual property; this can open new markets through buying a company's product line rather than the whole company

King David, the Democratic Leader

Israel had been led by a series of "judges", the charismatic warriors, priests and prophets whose influence was limited by their tribal structure of government. Samuel was the last of the judges, because the people began saying they needed a king just as the neighbouring countries. Samuel anointed Saul to be the first king.

Saul was a tall man, but the youngest son of a family in the small tribe of Benjamin. His first military victory consolidated his popular support before he was actually made king. Soon after, however, his impatience led Samuel to tell him that the kingship would leave his family. (Perhaps Shakespeare's *Macbeth* had the same experience, when told that Banquo's descendants would rule Scotland).

Later Samuel anointed David to become the second king, in a small ceremony only attended by David's family. David, too, was the youngest son in his family; his job was tending sheep. In fact, he was not invited to the ceremony with Samuel because David was so insignificant.

Saul remained king for many years. David was appointed as a musician for Saul, and also became an armour-bearer for the king.

Everyone has heard the story of David and Goliath, the Philistine giant who challenged Israel to a one-on-one fight. Although David was working for King Saul, he also still had to tend his family's sheep while his older brothers served in the army. David endured scorn from his brothers, and from Saul, before he could persuade the king to let him fight Goliath on his own terms: a slingshot against a sword, spear and javelin.

Some commentators point out, with 20-20 hindsight, that the smart money would have been bet on David's victory. The stone from his slingshot could reach Goliath from afar; it seems Goliath was intent on a toe-to-toe melee. Their analysis misses the point that no other Israelite soldier had thought of this tactic. The book of I Samuel portrays David as the only brave Israelite in the face of Goliath's challenge. One lesson in leadership, however, is that it pays to be smarter as well. If you cannot win the game, try changing the rules.

David was rewarded with a position in King Saul's army as a commander. David's successes led to conflict with Saul, however. When people sang "Saul has slain thousands, and David has slain tens of thousands", Saul felt the pangs of jealousy. (Much later, when General Joab served King David, Joab remembered to invite David to finish conquering a city. Joab did not want to steal honour from his king).

David refused the first offer of marriage that he received. King Saul wanted David to marry his eldest daughter. David turned her down because he was a lowly commoner. David said much the same when offered a younger daughter by Saul, but agreed when he was advised that it would be unwise to turn down the king's offer twice.

The book of I Samuel says that King Saul honoured David and sent him on military expeditions so the Philistines would eventually kill David. David took advantage of these opportunities by winning victories, no doubt developing his skills as a leader and as a guerrilla warrior.

David also planned for a future project, which he would not complete. David realized that he had built a palace for himself, but neglected to build a temple for worship. God told him to leave that task to his successor. David did, however, begin amassing the materials for the temple. He also left careful instructions that this project should be completed after his death (I Chron. 22, note verses 7-10 especially).

David used several "resuscitation" techniques for his own survival and reign. He set specific objectives: after staying alive while King Saul pursued him, he switched to establishing peace through strength against foreign aggressors after he gained the throne.

David "kept it real" by taking wise advice when it was given. He did not try to make every decision or to stifle criticism. By his military successes, David "built his personal brand" in the eyes of the people; even if he did not intend to supplant King Saul. By his courageous personal leadership in battle, David developed and retained a loyal cadre of trusted, battle-hardened soldiers who were loyal to him and helped him achieve his goals.

Chapter 11 – Phase Three: NURSING: The Corporate Man

Phase Three: The Nursing Stage: The Corporate Man

The nursing phase provides therapy for the patient. A physiotherapist or occupational therapist becomes involved at this stage, training the patient to strengthen weakened muscles or to learn how to adapt after the traumatic surgery.

The corporate patient must develop new internal strategies and learn to work in new ways. One example is the development of an improved corporate culture. The company must find a balance among an aggressive push for sales growth, the on-going pursuit of efficiencies, the development of new capabilities or products, and a steady rise in quality.

Change Management Leadership for the Nursing Phase

This phase continues to build a strong management team, but the philosophy must percolate down and transform the corporate culture. More than in the previous phases, everyone in the company must begin to understand and buy into the new approach: Whether the immediate tasks are cutting costs, expanding markets or developing innovations, the corporation must be ready to adapt as the world changes around it.

Change management leadership in this phase must model the type of manager who can plan, act and react. This leader must also deliberately build a management team able to continue adapting and improving into the future.

Twin Approaches During the Resuscitation Phase

The twin approaches for the nursing stage involve "philosophy" and "action".

Nursing a Corporation through Philosophy

This section is appropriate whether a company has narrowly escaped bankruptcy by implementing the first two phases of "Corporate Turnaround", or for an organization that wants to grow stronger, more robust, and more able to withstand difficulties in the future.

Some might call this a process to change an organization's "corporate culture", or a person's "belief system". To pursue the analogy of a human patient, suppose a lung cancer patient had a tumour removed. Surely this patient would receive counselling about the importance of quitting smoking before being released from hospital. The patient must truly believe in the importance of this difficult step, to have any hope of changing his or her harmful habits.

So too the organization must adopt three vital beliefs:
- To seek, evaluate and adopt new concepts and methods

- To appreciate on-going change, both internally-generated and externally-imposed
- To accept that some projects will fail, but that this does not mean the people or company are failures.

These beliefs may seem trivial, or they may challenge your organization's preconceived notions.

Seek New Concepts and Methods

Let's explore an example: how to communicate news to your employees? Innovative methods have been adopted over time:

- Hold face-to-face meetings: the CEO with top executives; executives with their direct reports; and so on to managers, supervisors and front-line workers.
- Make telephone calls: one-to-one calls might be replaced by conference calls or the use of a speakerphone in a boardroom.
- Post notices on bulletin boards
- Print a newsletter or a personal letter, and then send it by regular mail
- Send an e-mail to the list of all employees
- Post the information on an intra-net site
- Post the information on an employee Facebook page
- Tweet the information via Twitter

Each method has advantages or disadvantages. Holding face-to-face meetings requires people to be in the same location, and takes a lot of time just to set up those meetings. Individual telephone calls save on travel time, but conference calls take time to arrange and start.

For sensitive announcements, e-mail may be the best choice for speed and cost. It does require a cultural change: that all employees will monitor their e-mail regularly.

Appreciate On-going Change

External changes are inevitable. New competitors arise; familiar competitors develop new products, services or methods of delivery. Customers become more demanding or, even worse, demand fewer of your company's products.

Front-line workers will need to accept changes to improve their efficiency, quality or effectiveness. Upper management must constantly review and revise strategies, products and pricing.

Resistance is futile; it just makes the electric wire hotter. Companies that embrace and appreciate on-going change will find ways to benefit from those changes.

Accept Some Failure

The great example of successful failure is Thomas Edison, whose thousands of unsuccessful light bulbs led to one success with the tungsten filament in a vacuum. He saw each "failure" as a step toward success.

If your organization imposes a punishment for each failed attempt, it trains the employees to avoid innovating. People will do what is rewarded and avoid what is punished. Assuming that the executives accept the need for on-going change, then they must implement a culture that rewards attempts to make improvements.

Nursing a Corporation through Action

Corporate action must follow from the philosophical changes. Make innovation a priority in the budget and for the executive team. Actively seek new opportunities; especially try to transform setbacks or obstacles into new products, services or markets. Reward innovators and avoid punishing those who try but fall short of success; treat these situations as lessons rather than as failures.

Changing a Corporate Culture

The term "corporate culture" refers to the combination of values, practices, beliefs and assumptions that its employees follow. A typical small business is entrepreneurial as it begins: each employee looks for new sales or revenue opportunities; perhaps each has the authority to sign up new customers and begin servicing their needs. By contrast, in a well-established bank, a regional vice-president may need to observe strict lending limits and to refer many opportunities to an executive vice-president for approval.

An organization gets into a crisis because its culture allowed it to happen. Heroic efforts to cut costs or increase market share may keep the corporate afloat, but a flawed corporate culture will undermine long-term efforts at recovery and growth.

An important goal of the Nursing phase is to change the corporate culture. Almost always this change involves making people welcome external challenges by embracing and creating changes to obsolete procedures or outdated targets and goals.

One way to succeed is to develop "Stakeholder Relationship Management" skills. This has parallels to "Customer Relationship Management", in which the sales executive seeks to know the customer's needs, desires and problems.

The "Stakeholder RM" process considers all the stakeholders when planning a change. Who are these people?

- Those directly affected: employees, customers, suppliers and vendors
- The change agents: staff, management and contracted experts
- The decision makers, who are usually the shareholders, the directors, and C-level executives
- Those indirectly affected; one example is an employee's spouse who must make

adjustments if the employee has new travel duties or work shifts

The "Stakeholder RM" process first must identify the stakeholders, and then their ambitions and concerns. This knowledge helps the corporate transformation leader decide how to achieve the corporate goal as well as meeting the needs of the various stakeholders.

This RM knowledge also drives the culture change, because all the stakeholders need to make the transition.

Let's give one example of a change in the corporate culture. An "old school" middle manager may be accustomed to reviewing customer requirements before started production. Based on experience and knowledge, that manager might overrule the sales and design team, saying "These custom features will be too expensive. Use this standard option, since it is profitable for us and almost what the customer wanted". The corporate transformation, however, identified customization as the precise service most required to land and retain new business. How can this stakeholder – the middle manager – adapt after losing the power to veto or revise summarily? Perhaps the new role is to review the price and the schedule; possibly to obtain an exemption from profitability requirements for a new customer's first order.

The Apostle Paul as the Corporate Man

The apostle Paul may be considered an exemplary "corporate man". This section will begin with a brief telling of his career, and then see how he was an excellent corporate role model.

Paul's Resume

Paul first appears in Acts 8:1, he goes by the name "Saul" because he wants to highlight his Jewish heritage and his strong support for a fundamentalist form of Judaism. In fact, he requested and obtained a "bounty hunter" license from the Jewish High Priest to arrest Christians.

While hunting Christians, Paul experienced a miracle on the road to Damascus. He converted to Christianity, met with some disciples, and spent quite some time preparing for his ministry.

He later called himself "Paul" to reflect his Roman citizenship and his career choice to become a missionary to Gentiles. (It is believed that Paul had been born in the Roman city of Tarsus, to which he returned from Jerusalem when he was first persecuted).

Barnabas became a mentor to Paul. They spent a year working in Antioch, mainly teaching Greek-speaking Jewish converts. Later Paul received support and credentials from the "senior" Christian leaders in Antioch. (Many Christian leaders had left their first headquarters in Jerusalem due to persecution such as delivered by Saul, and settled in Antioch).

They sent Paul, and his selected team members, on missionary journeys. His partners included Barnabas, Silas, Mark and Timothy at various times. Paul insisted on loyalty and effort: he rejected Mark at one time for deserting the team during an early mission.

Paul balanced his principles and practical tactics. Early Christianity began with Jews, who continued to follow the laws of Moses in their daily lives. As Gentiles embraced Christianity, questions arose as to whether they too would be required to keep kosher and follow all the Jewish regulations. Paul was a firm advocate that no, the Gentiles should not be made to practice Judaism as a pre-requisite for becoming Christian. On the other hand, he ensured that Timothy was circumcised in preparation for joining Paul's missionary team. Paul did not want to fight unnecessary battles with Jewish leaders about his team members; he knew there would be more important issues on the line.

Paul built for the future, training a variety of helpers. Timothy may be the best known, since Paul wrote two letters to him. These letters advised Timothy how to lead one congregation.

Paul's many letters to individual churches gave instructions for conducting services and for resolving disputes. As well, these letters provided much of the doctrinal foundation for the entire Christian movement.

Paul as a Corporate Role Model

Paul exhibited a number of special traits that make him an excellent role model for a turnaround situation.

He requested and received top-level support, whether from Jewish authorities or from Christian leaders.

He took the time to train and learn from more experienced people such as Barnabas, whom he later "outranked".

Paul recruited top-notch subordinates. He mentored them during his work, eventually installing people like Timothy to lead congregations themselves. When he delegated such responsibility, he also continued to support these "junior executives" as needed.

He did not succeed in every aspect of every mission. As noted, he was disappointed in Mark; but later asked him to return as Paul's assistant. Paul did not always escape from prison; but he used his jail time to further his primary goal of bringing the Gospel to everyone.

Paul was willing to confront, but also could wield a variety of diplomatic tools. The letters to the Corinthian church show that he could name problems and strongly recommend specific solutions. Yet he could wheedle and cajole; his letter to Philemon is a model of such a style. Take Philemon 1: 19, for example: "...I will repay it; although I do not mention that you owe me your very life" (in the sense of his eternal soul's salvation).

Paul was also instrumental in changing the "corporate culture" of the early church. While Jesus (Mark 7:24-30) and Peter (Acts 10:1 through 11:18) did reach out to Gentiles on occasion, Paul's missionary journeys were heavily tilted toward Gentiles. This helped to change the early

Christian movement from a Jewish sect to a global and multi-racial religion.

Paul made himself a practical, living example this new culture. He had been a devout and observant follower of Judaism, but then spent much of his ministry with Gentiles. No doubt he had kept kosher as "…a Hebrew of the Hebrews; as touching the Law, a Pharisee". (Phil. 3: 5). However, Paul later was willing to eat anything, even what Judaism condemned as unclean. (Rom. 14:1-3 and 14: 14-15). Paul also argued convincingly to promote this new cultural view, even to Peter who was the acknowledged leader of the Christian faith. (Gal. 2: 11-21).

This concludes the chapters explaining "Corporate Turnaround". However, every book dealing with a Christian approach must ask "what would Jesus do?" Indeed, Jesus provided leadership in a wide variety of situations. The next chapter selects examples from the life and ministry of Jesus in which he embodies the methods of "Corporate Turnaround".

Chapter 12 – The Dimensional Shift: The Greatest Leader

Dimensional Shift: Jesus, the Greatest Leader

We have considered the plight of business organizations in distress, and recommended the three-phase Corporate Turnaround strategy to "cure" this "patient". As well, we have highlighted several Biblical leaders who provided strong examples.

The Bible demonstrates, however, that Jesus was the greatest leader. He took time for his own needs, yet set a higher priority on serving others. He dealt with individuals whether they were respected or despised. He trained teams, trusted them with tasks, and also worked with large crowds.

How Jesus Met Various Needs

Several Gospel stories mention that Jesus would go away by himself to pray. This was his way of ensuring he was ready for his next tasks: whether to cross a lake or to take up his cross on Good Friday.

But when Jesus returned to the disciples, he took time to deal with their problems. When he walked across the lake, which terrified his disciples, Jesus calmed their fears (Mark 6: 46- 52). After praying in Gethsemane, Jesus encouraged his disciples to stay awake, but also healed one of the people who came to arrest him – a servant whose ear was cut off in the very brief melee. (Matt. 26: 36-54 and Luke 22: 39-51).

One time, Jesus fell asleep in a boat; he nearly slept through the storm that threatened to capsize the vessel. When Jesus was awakened in the boat, he first calmed the storm, and then his distraught disciples. (Matt. 8: 23-27).

Jesus Worked with a Variety of People

Jesus called Levi, a despised tax collector, as a disciple (Mark 2: 13-17). Jesus admitted that Levi might not have started out as a "righteous" person, but that doctors go to sick people rather than to the healthy. (Modern medical practice would, of course, encourage healthy people to get see their doctors for check-ups; Jesus might agree, since he did attend synagogues and he spent all his time on "his Father's business").

Jesus healed the daughter of a Greek Syro-Phoenician woman. A good Jewish rabbi should not have spoken to an unrelated woman, let alone a Gentile woman. He teased her about this, but her humble reply allowed Jesus to grant the healing miracle (Mark 7: 26-30).

But Jesus also worked with respected Jewish leaders. One example was Nicodemus, a member of the Sanhedrin, the council of Pharisees in Jerusalem (John 3).

How Jesus Worked with Small Teams and Large Crowds

Jesus sent the twelve disciples on one mission (Luke 9: 1-10). Later he sent a team of 72 (Luke 10: 1-18). In both cases, Jesus:
- Gave instructions and authority to the team
- Debriefed the teams after they returned

Immediately after the first mission noted above, Jesus took the disciples to the town of Bethsaida for their debriefing. However, "crowds" followed Jesus for his teaching and his miracles of healing. Jesus gave the crowds what they wanted; but it took so long that evening was approaching. The disciples suggested dispersing the crowd, but Jesus empowered the disciples to feed them all…with just five loaves of bread and two fish, probably the spares meal the disciples had expected for themselves. (Luke 9: 11-17).

Let's note that the disciples had just performed miracles of healing in Luke 9: 1-10, but very quickly failed to recognize the opportunity to do well in a different situation, in Luke 9: 11-17. As business leaders, do we fail to recognize opportunities when they wear unfamiliar disguises?

The situation at Bethsaida was just one example of how Jesus combined opportunities to teach and to do good deeds. Whether some people joined the crowd simply for a chance at healing, or whether the majority wanted to hear a famous preacher, Jesus took time to do both.

Jesus and the Corporate Turnaround Process

Let's consider what Jesus might do as a business leader, executing the Corporate Turnaround strategy.

Jesus in the Surgery Phase: Decisive Leadership

Surgery is a drastic medical treatment. Jesus took drastic action at least twice.

In a Gentile area, Jesus met two men who were possessed by demons. Jesus sent the demons from these people into a nearby herd of pigs, which then ran down a steep slope into a lake and drowned (Matt. 8:28-34). As a leader, Jesus quickly assessed the situation, accepted a suggestion – from the demons – and then took decisive action. The herdsmen, of course, reported what happened. This must have been a serious economic blow to the farmer(s). In fact, the whole town begged Jesus to leave, possibly fearing that this Jew would eliminate more of their non-kosher food.

Once, when Jesus visited Jerusalem, he was shocked and angered by the businesses being run in the temple. There are differing opinions as to whether the "currency exchange" operations and the livestock sales were cheating the pilgrims, or whether Jesus just felt it was not appropriate to transact business in the courtyard of the temple. Regardless, Jesus made a whip, drove out the animals as well as the business people, and overturned the tables where the coins had been stacked. Again, Jesus took quick, decisive and unpopular action. He saw beyond the accepted practices and insisted on change.

Jesus in the Resuscitation Phase: Compassionate but Fair

Jesus dealt with Pilate in a way unusual for prisoners to treat their judges. Jesus had refused to "mount a vigorous defence", as is normal in modern trials. This unnerved Pilate, particularly when Jesus was accused of claiming to be "the Son of God". As a Roman, Pilate's religion had many stories of demigods, such as Heracles, Orpheus and Phaeton. From Pilate's perspective, it was entirely possible that he might be judging a powerful son of a god. Yet Jesus reassured Pilate: "The one who handed me over to you is guilty of a greater sin" (John 19: 1-11). If Pilate had been listening carefully, perhaps he would not have felt quite so reassured, since Jesus did not completely exonerate Pilate. But Jesus did display compassion and fairness, even when he was being mistreated.

Jesus in the Nursing Phase: Building a Better Future

Let's focus on what Jesus did for his disciples after his resurrection. One example comes in Luke 24:13-33. Two disciples were walking to Emmaus, a town seven miles from Jerusalem. They were in despair because Jesus had been killed; and confused because of a rumour that his tomb was empty. These disciples did not recognize their fellow traveller, who seemed to know nothing of current events but everything about the prophecies concerning a suffering servant who would be the Messiah.

John's gospel records several instances where Jesus appeared to some disciples. Each time the visit inspires faith. Yet Jesus took time especially for Peter, who had betrayed Jesus during the trials (John 18:15-18 and 25-27, and John 21: 15-19). Jesus had seen Peter's potential to be a great leader, and made sure that Peter would be up for the challenge despite his earlier failure.

In both these situations, Jesus recognized the emotional state his disciples were experiencing. He took the time to craft a response to fit their needs, and these responses also empowered those disciples to develop and continue growing into the roles they were to play in the future.

Cultural Change

Let's consider what Jesus did with regard to implementing cultural change. As Paul would later do, Jesus promoted cultural change by word and deed.

Jesus Spoke for Cultural Change

Anabaptists quote Jesus' Sermon on the Mount (Matt. 5 through 7) as the call for cultural change. One example will suffice. In the Torah, Moses limited vengeance to "life for life, eye for eye, tooth for tooth..." (Ex. 21: 23-24). Jesus said, "You have heard it said, 'An eye for an eye and a tooth for a tooth'; but I say...whoever smites you on your right cheek, turn to him the other also". (Matt. 5: 38-39).

Here, Jesus was calling for a radical re-thinking of the culture of vengeance and retributive justice.

Jesus Acted for Cultural Change

In Jesus' day, a devout Jew would have no dealings with Samaritans (if it could be avoided), even though they had common ancestry and similar religious views. Nor would a righteous man speak with an unknown woman, since it would appear that he was soliciting a prostitute.

Yet when Jesus travelled through Samaria, he struck up a conversation with the Samaritan woman at the well near Sychar. Both she, and later his disciples, were amazed that Jesus would hold this conversation. Jesus used this conversation to begin a two-day missionary effort in Sychar, demonstrating that his message was not confined to "proper Jews" from Judea and Galilee, and also that some cultural conventions could be overturned. (John 4: 1-40).

Jesus Provided Leadership to Meet the Need

You may recall that the "Situational Leadership" theory suggested that the leader should use the style appropriate to the subordinate's capabilities. Jesus, for example, taught crowds with parables about common events such as seeking lost sheep; but he captured the attention of the educated Pharisee, Nicodemus, with the phrase "must be born again". He showed compassion to the ill, but drove money-changers out of the Temple.

The Corporate Turnaround Strategy advises that different styles are required in the different phases of Surgery, Resuscitation and Nursing. When Jesus began his ministry, he called specific disciples and taught the crowds. At the end of his ministry, he as with crowds on Palm Sunday but spent his final free hours with only the disciples in the Last Supper.

It would be tempting to quote the end of John's gospel: "Jesus did many other things as well". (John 21:25). Let's leave this chapter, regardless of the many other examples of the leadership of Jesus. The next chapter briefly concludes this book.

Chapter 13 – Conclusion: Managing Change: Tested and True

Change Management Leadership and Biblical Examples

Leaders, Managers and Leadership

We know that that people look for leaders to guide them out of difficulties. We briefly reviewed the leadership theories proposed throughout the 20th century. We found historic examples of a few of the best and brightest leaders in politics, business and religion.

Often the best leaders create or rescue nations, corporations or religious movements. They promoted their vision of change by combining inspiring words and exemplary deeds.

Business managers often focus on the status quo: maintain sales; expand into the obvious markets; audit the accounting system to ensure compliance. This is a limited type of leadership, since it does not generate a new vision or new energy for the organization.

Leadership is needed for bold and difficult tasks: to make radical improvements: to rescue an organization in a crisis; or to transform a corporation that failed to adapt to changing circumstances.

Corporate Turnaround Requires Change Management

When a modern corporation is in crisis, it needs three types of rescue. The immediate threat is bankruptcy or insolvency; the solution is surgical cost cutting. Soon thereafter, cash flow and sales must be resuscitated through aggressive marketing. Long-term survival requires nursing care with a transformation of the corporate culture. That transformation is needed in order to avoid falling into the same trap as led to the recent crisis.

Corporate turnaround is not a quick-and-easy fix. It is a major change for an organization, requiring a leader skilled in change management.

Leadership is about Character as well as Skill

Beyond having skills, a leader must possess character traits that inspire their followers.

Many of the best leaders…those with exceptional personalities…are found in the Bible.

Tested and True Business Management and Biblical Management

Corporate Turnaround's three-phase approach can be summarized in a table as follows:

	Phase 1	Phase 2	Phase 3
Phase Name	Surgery	Resuscitation	Nursing
Process	Cut costs	Develop sales	Plan for growth
Leadership	Autocratic	Democratic	Corporate
Primary Goal	Avoid bankruptcy	Profitability	Expansion
Secondary Goal	Focus on core	Increase marketing	New corporate culture for growth
Time Frame	A few months	Under one year	More than one year
Biblical Leader	Joshua	King David	Paul the apostle
...his Task	Conquest	Consolidate and Plan	Marketing and Mentoring
...his Style	Autocratic	Democratic	Spiritual
Jesus	Exorcism; Temple business	Compassion for Pilate, his judge	Dealing with the apostles after His resurrection

There are no solid edges between these phases. Rather, the turnaround CEO should transition from one to the next as the current measures take effect and the business improves. For example, Phase 1's emphasis on cost cutting and improving cash flow should shift to looking for sales revenue in Phase 2; but the business must not allow cash flow to slow down due to delayed receivables or increased inventories.

Corporate turnaround is a difficult process. It requires serious attention and energy, particularly from the leader. There may be moments of excitement; there definitely will be hours of work. People might thank you; some will certainly be unhappy if their pet projects are cancelled or their work habits changed.

The Biblical leaders serve as reminders that shared cultural understandings, shared goals, and shared vision for the future can unify an organization and focus the energies of many people, thus leading to success. These Biblical leaders displayed very different management styles but ultimately worked for a shared goal.

Each of these leaders addressed the most important issues of their day. Joshua had to rally a group of tribes after their previous leader's death, and then conquer the land they had been promised. David achieved his nation's military successes, and then began planning to consolidate their religious practices in a new temple. The Apostle Paul spread the Christian message throughout the Roman world, and was the key leader in changing this new religion from its Jewish roots to an international and interracial movement. He also mentored the next generation of leaders.

Jesus was the great example of leadership, relating to a variety of people in whatever ways they required. Jesus was decisive and compassionate; comfortable with individuals and with crowds; focussed on the moment and also looking to the future. No finer example of leadership is available to any leader in any situation.

www.ingramcontent.com/pod-product-compliance
Lightning Source LLC
Chambersburg PA
CBHW071120210326
41519CB00020B/6354